The Actors' Ch

The Actors' Choosing

✡

Edited by
STANLEY WELLS

LONG BARN BOOKS

PUBLISHED BY
LONG BARN BOOKS

Ebrington, Gloucestershire GL55 6NW

This collection first published in 1997
1 3 5 7 9 10 8 6 4 2

Set in 12/14.25pt Monotype Garamond
Printed and bound by Redwood Books, Trowbridge, Wiltshire

ISBN 0 952 8285 6 1

CONTENTS

✡

FOREWORD

✡

Great thanks are due to actors associated with the Royal Shakespeare Company for their willing and friendly co-operation in compiling this anthology. They were invited to choose passages from Shakespeare's plays which had especial appeal for them personally. Most but not all of these extracts of the actors' choosing come from roles in which they have themselves appeared. No attempt was made to direct them to particular plays, and it is a tribute to the richness and variety of Shakespeare, and to the opportunities that plays written from the beginning to the end of his career offer to actors, that this selection covers almost the entire canon of his work. The actors' choices have evoked in me powerful memories of great performances and productions over the years, and I am sure they will do the same for many readers. And even those unfamiliar with the Royal Shakespeare Company's work will find here a rewarding collection not only of some of Shakespeares finest speaches and scenes, but of those that exert the greatest appeal for the finest actors of our time.

Special thanks are due to Kathy Elgin, Publications Manager of the Royal Shakespeare Company, both for suggesting the book in the first place, and for practical assistance in bringing it into being.

S.W.

ROGER ALLAM

✡

Measure for Measure

Act III Scene 1

The Duke of Vienna, disguised as a friar, offers comfort to Claudio, condemned to death for fornication.

DUKE
So then, you hope of pardon from Lord Angelo?
CLAUDIO
The miserable have no other medicine
But only hope.
I've hope to live, and am prepared to die.
DUKE
Be absolute for death. Either death or life
Shall thereby be the sweeter. Reason thus with life.
If I do lose thee, I do lose a thing
That none but fools would keep. A breath thou art,
Servile to all the skyey influences
That dost this habitation where thou keep'st
Hourly afflict. Merely thou art death's fool,
For him thou labour'st by thy flight to shun,
And yet runn'st toward him still. Thou art not noble,
For all th'accommodations that thou bear'st
Are nursed by baseness. Thou'rt by no means valiant,
For thou dost fear the soft and tender fork

Of a poor worm. Thy best of rest is sleep,
And that thou oft provok'st, yet grossly fear'st
Thy death, which is no more. Thou art not thyself,
For thou exist'st on many a thousand grains
That issue out of dust. Happy thou art not,
For what thou hast not, still thou striv'st to get,
And what thou hast, forget'st. Thou art not certain,
For thy complexion shifts to strange effects
After the moon. If thou art rich, thou'rt poor,
For like an ass whose back with ingots bows,
Thou bear'st thy heavy riches but a journey,
And death unloads thee. Friend hast thou none,
For thine own bowels, which do call thee sire,
The mere effusion of thy proper loins,
Do curse the gout, serpigo, and the rheum,
For ending thee no sooner. Thou hast nor youth nor age,
But as it were an after-dinner's sleep
Dreaming on both; for all thy blessèd youth
Becomes as agèd, and doth beg the alms
Of palsied eld; and when thou art old and rich,
Thou hast neither heat, affection, limb, nor beauty,
To make thy riches pleasant. What's in this
That bears the name of life? Yet in this life
Lie hid more thousand deaths; yet death we fear
That makes these odds all even.

CLAUDIO I humbly thank you.
To sue to live, I find I seek to die,
And seeking death, find life. Let it come on.

Roger Allam played the Duke with the Royal Shakespeare Company in 1987

FRANCESCA ANNIS

✡

Romeo and Juliet

Act III Scene 2

Juliet looks forward to her wedding night.

Gallop apace, you fiery-footed steeds,
Towards Phoebus' lodging. Such a waggoner
As Phaëton would whip you to the west
And bring in cloudy night immediately.
Spread thy close curtain, love-performing night,
That runaways' eyes may wink, and Romeo
Leap to these arms untalked of and unseen.
Lovers can see to do their amorous rites
By their own beauties; or, if love be blind,
It best agrees with night. Come, civil night,
Thou sober-suited matron all in black,
And learn me how to lose a winning match
Played for a pair of stainless maidenhoods.
Hood my unmanned blood, bating in my cheeks,
With thy black mantle till strange love grown bold
Think true love acted simple modesty.
Come night, come Romeo; come, thou day in night,
For thou wilt lie upon the wings of night
Whiter than new snow on a raven's back.

Come, gentle night; come, loving, black-browed night,
Give me my Romeo, and when I shall die
Take him and cut him out in little stars,
And he will make the face of heaven so fine
That all the world will be in love with night
And pay no worship to the garish sun.
O, I have bought the mansion of a love
But not possessed it, and though I am sold,
Not yet enjoyed. So tedious is this day
As is the night before some festival
To an impatient child that hath new robes
And may not wear them.

Francesca Annis played Juliet with the Royal Shakespeare Company in 1977.

DES BARRIT

✡

The Comedy of Errors

Act III Scene 2

Luciana, mistaking Antipholus of Syracuse for her brother-in-law Antipholus of Ephesus, rebukes him to such effect that he falls in love with her.

LUCIANA

And may it be that you have quite forgot
 A husband's office? Shall, Antipholus,
Even in the spring of love thy love-springs rot?
 Shall love, in building, grow so ruinous?
If you did wed my sister for her wealth,
 Then for her wealth's sake use her with more kindness;
Or if you like elsewhere, do it by stealth:
 Muffle your false love with some show of blindness.
Let not my sister read it in your eye.
 Be not thy tongue thy own shame's orator.
Look sweet, speak fair, become disloyalty;
 Apparel vice like virtue's harbinger.
Bear a fair presence, though your heart be tainted:
 Teach sin the carriage of a holy saint.
Be secret-false. What need she be acquainted?
 What simple thief brags of his own attaint?

'Tis double wrong to truant with your bed,
    And let her read it in thy looks at board.
Shame hath a bastard fame, well managèd;
    Ill deeds is doubled with an evil word.
Alas, poor women, make us but believe—
    Being compact of credit—that you love us.
Though others have the arm, show us the sleeve.
    We in your motion turn, and you may move us.
Then, gentle brother, get you in again.
    Comfort my sister, cheer her, call her wife:
'Tis holy sport to be a little vain
    When the sweet breath of flattery conquers strife.

ANTIPHOLUS OF SYRACUSE

Sweet mistress—what your name is else I know not,
    Nor by what wonder you do hit of mine.
Less in your knowledge and your grace you show not
    Than our earth's wonder, more than earth divine.
Teach me, dear creature, how to think and speak.
    Lay open to my earthy gross conceit,
Smothered in errors, feeble, shallow, weak,
    The folded meaning of your words' deceit.
Against my soul's pure truth why labour you
    To make it wander in an unknown field?
Are you a god? Would you create me new?
    Transform me, then, and to your power I'll yield.
But if that I am I, then well I know
    Your weeping sister is no wife of mine,
Nor to her bed no homage do I owe.
    Far more, far more, to you do I decline.
O, train me not, sweet mermaid, with thy note
    To drown me in thy sister's flood of tears.
Sing, siren, for thyself, and I will dote.

Spread o'er the silver waves thy golden hairs,
And as a bed I'll take them, and there lie,
And in that glorious supposition think
He gains by death that hath such means to die.
Let love, being light, be drownèd if she sink.

LUCIANA
What, are you mad, that you do reason so?

ANTIPHOLUS OF SYRACUSE
Not mad, but mated—how, I do not know.

LUCIANA
It is a fault that springeth from your eye.

ANTIPHOLUS OF SYRACUSE
For gazing on your beams, fair sun, being by.

LUCIANA
Gaze where you should, and that will clear your sight.

ANTIPHOLUS OF SYRACUSE
As good to wink, sweet love, as look on night.

LUCIANA
Why call you me 'love'? Call my sister so.

ANTIPHOLUS OF SYRACUSE
Thy sister's sister.

LUCIANA That's my sister.

ANTIPHOLUS OF SYRACUSE No,
It is thyself, mine own self's better part,
Mine eye's clear eye, my dear heart's dearer heart,
My food, my fortune, and my sweet hope's aim,
My sole earth's heaven, and my heaven's claim.

LUCIANA
All this my sister is, or else should be.

ANTIPHOLUS OF SYRACUSE
Call thyself sister, sweet, for I am thee.
Thee will I love, and with thee lead my life.

Thou hast no husband yet, nor I no wife.
Give me thy hand.

LUCIANA O soft, sir, hold you still;
I'll fetch my sister to get her good will.
. . .

ANTIPHOLUS OF SYRACUSE
There's none but witches do inhabit here,
And therefore 'tis high time that I were hence.
She that doth call me husband, even my soul
Doth for a wife abhor. But her fair sister,
Possessed with such a gentle sovereign grace,
Of such enchanting presence and discourse,
Hath almost made me traitor to myself.
But lest myself be guilty to self-wrong,
I'll stop mine ears against the mermaid's song.

Des Barrit played both Antipholus of Syracuse and Antipholus of Ephesus with the Royal Shakespeare Company in 1990.

SIMON RUSSELL BEALE

✡

Richard III

Act IV Scene 4

King Richard tries to persuade Queen Elizabeth, widow of King Edward IV, to encourage her daughter to marry him.

KING RICHARD
Stay, madam. I must talk a word with you.
QUEEN ELIZABETH
I have no more sons of the royal blood
For thee to slaughter. For my daughters, Richard,
They shall be praying nuns, not weeping queens,
And therefore level not to hit their lives.
KING RICHARD
You have a daughter called Elizabeth,
Virtuous and fair, royal and gracious.
QUEEN ELIZABETH
And must she die for this? O let her live,
And I'll corrupt her manners, stain her beauty,
Slander myself as false to Edward's bed,
Throw over her the veil of infamy.
So she may live unscarred of bleeding slaughter,
I will confess she was not Edward's daughter.
KING RICHARD
Wrong not her birth. She is a royal princess.

QUEEN ELIZABETH
To save her life I'll say she is not so.
KING RICHARD
Her life is safest only in her birth.
QUEEN ELIZABETH
And only in that safety died her brothers.
KING RICHARD
Lo, at their births good stars were opposite.
QUEEN ELIZABETH
No, to their lives ill friends were contrary.
KING RICHARD
All unavoided is the doom of destiny—
QUEEN ELIZABETH
True, when avoided grace makes destiny.
My babes were destined to a fairer death,
If grace had blessed thee with a fairer life.
KING RICHARD
Madam, so thrive I in my enterprise
And dangerous success of bloody wars,
As I intend more good to you and yours
Than ever you or yours by me were harmed.
QUEEN ELIZABETH
What good is covered with the face of heaven,
To be discovered, that can do me good?
KING RICHARD
Th'advancement of your children, gentle lady.
QUEEN ELIZABETH
Up to some scaffold, there to lose their heads.
KING RICHARD
Unto the dignity and height of fortune,
The high imperial type of this earth's glory.

QUEEN ELIZABETH

Flatter my sorrow with report of it.
Tell me what state, what dignity, what honour,
Canst thou demise to any child of mine?

KING RICHARD

Even all I have—ay, and myself and all,
Will I withal endow a child of thine,
So in the Lethe of thy angry soul
Thou drown the sad remembrance of those wrongs,
Which thou supposest I have done to thee.

QUEEN ELIZABETH

Be brief, lest that the process of thy kindness
Last longer telling than thy kindness' date.

KING RICHARD

Then know that, from my soul, I love thy daughter.

QUEEN ELIZABETH

My daughter's mother thinks that with her soul.

KING RICHARD

What do you think?

QUEEN ELIZABETH

That thou dost love my daughter from thy soul;
So from thy soul's love didst thou love her brothers,
And from my heart's love I do thank thee for it.

KING RICHARD

Be not so hasty to confound my meaning.
I mean, that with my soul I love thy daughter,
And do intend to make her queen of England.

QUEEN ELIZABETH

Well then, who dost thou mean shall be her king?

KING RICHARD

Even he that makes her queen. Who else should be?

QUEEN ELIZABETH
What, thou?
KING RICHARD Even so. How think you of it?
QUEEN ELIZABETH
How canst thou woo her?
KING RICHARD That would I learn of you,
As one being best acquainted with her humour.
QUEEN ELIZABETH
And wilt thou learn of me?
KING RICHARD Madam, with all my heart.
QUEEN ELIZABETH
Send to her, by the man that slew her brothers,
A pair of bleeding hearts; thereon engrave
'Edward'and 'York' then haply will she weep.
Therefore present to her—as sometimes Margaret
Did to thy father, steeped in Rutland's blood—
A handkerchief which, say to her, did drain
The purple sap from her sweet brother's body,
And bid her wipe her weeping eyes withal.
If this inducement move her not to love,
Send her a letter of thy noble deeds.
Tell her thou mad'st away her uncle Clarence,
Her uncle Rivers—ay, and for her sake
Mad'st quick conveyance with her good aunt Anne.
KING RICHARD
You mock me, madam. This is not the way
To win your daughter.
QUEEN ELIZABETH There is no other way,
Unless thou couldst put on some other shape,
And not be Richard, that hath done all this.
KING RICHARD
Infer fair England's peace by this alliance.

QUEEN ELIZABETH
Which she shall purchase with still-lasting war.
KING RICHARD
Tell her the King, that may command, entreats.
QUEEN ELIZABETH
That at her hands which the King's King forbids.
KING RICHARD
Say she shall be a high and mighty queen.
QUEEN ELIZABETH
To vail the title, as her mother doth.
KING RICHARD
Say I will love her everlastingly.
QUEEN ELIZABETH
But how long shall that title 'ever' last?
KING RICHARD
Sweetly in force unto her fair life's end.
QUEEN ELIZABETH
But how long fairly shall her sweet life last?
KING RICHARD
As long as heaven and nature lengthens it.
QUEEN ELIZABETH
As long as hell and Richard likes of it.
KING RICHARD
Say I, her sovereign, am her subject love.
QUEEN ELIZABETH
But she, your subject, loathes such sovereignty.
KING RICHARD
Be eloquent in my behalf to her.
QUEEN ELIZABETH
An honest tale speeds best being plainly told.
KING RICHARD
Then plainly to her tell my loving tale.

QUEEN ELIZABETH
Plain and not honest is too harsh a style.
KING RICHARD
Your reasons are too shallow and too quick.
QUEEN ELIZABETH
O no, my reasons are too deep and dead—
Too deep and dead, poor infants, in their graves.
KING RICHARD
Harp not on that string, madam. That is past.
QUEEN ELIZABETH
Harp on it still shall I, till heart-strings break.
KING RICHARD
Now by my George, my garter, and my crown—
QUEEN ELIZABETH
Profaned, dishonoured, and the third usurped.
KING RICHARD
I swear—
QUEEN ELIZABETH By nothing, for this is no oath.
Thy George, profaned, hath lost his holy honour;
Thy garter, blemished, pawned his lordly virtue;
Thy crown, usurped, disgraced his kingly glory.
If something thou wouldst swear to be believed,
Swear then by something that thou hast not wronged.
KING RICHARD
Then by myself—
QUEEN ELIZABETH Thy self is self-misused.
KING RICHARD
Now by the world—
QUEEN ELIZABETH 'Tis full of thy foul wrongs.
KING RICHARD
My father's death—

QUEEN ELIZABETH Thy life hath that dishonoured.

KING RICHARD
Why then, by God—

QUEEN ELIZABETH God's wrong is most of all.
If thou didst fear to break an oath with him,
The unity the King my husband made
Thou hadst not broken, nor my brothers died.
If thou hadst feared to break an oath by him,
Th' imperial metal circling now thy head
Had graced the tender temples of my child,
And both the princes had been breathing here,
Which now—two tender bedfellows for dust—
Thy broken faith hath made the prey for worms.
What canst thou swear by now?

KING RICHARD The time to come.

QUEEN ELIZABETH
That thou hast wrongèd in the time o'erpast,
For I myself have many tears to wash
Hereafter time, for time past wronged by thee.
The children live, whose fathers thou hast slaughtered—
Ungoverned youth, to wail it in their age.
The parents live, whose children thou hast butchered—
Old barren plants, to wail it with their age.
Swear not by time to come, for that thou hast
Misused ere used, by times ill-used o'erpast.

KING RICHARD
As I intend to prosper and repent,
So thrive I in my dangerous affairs
Of hostile arms—myself myself confound,
Heaven and fortune bar me happy hours,
Day yield me not thy light nor night thy rest;

Be opposite, all planets of good luck,
To my proceeding—if, with dear heart's love,
Immaculate devotion, holy thoughts,
I tender not thy beauteous, princely daughter.
In her consists my happiness and thine.
Without her follows—to myself and thee,
Herself, the land, and many a Christian soul—
Death, desolation, ruin, and decay.
It cannot be avoided but by this;
It will not be avoided but by this.
Therefore, good-mother—I must call you so—
Be the attorney of my love to her.
Plead what I will be, not what I have been;
Not my deserts, but what I will deserve.
Urge the necessity and state of times,
And be not peevish-fond in great designs.

QUEEN ELIZABETH
Shall I be tempted of the devil thus?

KING RICHARD
Ay, if the devil tempt you to do good.

QUEEN ELIZABETH
Shall I forget myself to be myself?

KING RICHARD
Ay, if yourself's remembrance wrong yourself.

QUEEN ELIZABETH Yet thou didst kill my children.

KING RICHARD
But in your daughter's womb I bury them,
Where, in that nest of spicery, they will breed
Selves of themselves, to your recomfiture.

QUEEN ELIZABETH
Shall I go win my daughter to thy will?

KING RICHARD

And be a happy mother by the deed.

QUEEN ELIZABETH

I go. Write to me very shortly,
And you shall understand from me her mind.

KING RICHARD

Bear her my true love's kiss,

He kisses her

and so farewell—

Exit Elizabeth

Relenting fool, and shallow, changing woman.

Simon Russell Beale played Richard III with the Royal Shakespeare Company in 1992.

CHERYL CAMPBELL

✡

Macbeth

Act I Scene 5

Lady Macbeth reads a letter from her husband.

Enter Lady Macbeth, with a letter

LADY MACBETH (*reading*) 'They met me in the day of success,and I have learned by the perfect'st report they have more in them than mortal knowledge. When I burned in desire to question them further, they made themselves air, into which they vanished. Whiles I stood rapt in the wonder of it came missives from the King, who all-hailed me "Thane of Cawdor", by which title before these weird sisters saluted me, and referred me to the coming on of time with "Hail, King that shalt be!" This have I thought good to deliver thee, my dearest partner of greatness, that thou mightst not lose the dues of rejoicing by being ignorant of what greatness is promised thee. Lay it to thy heart, and farewell.'

Glamis thou art, and Cawdor, and shalt be
What thou art promised. Yet do I fear thy nature.
It is too full o'th' milk of human kindness
To catch the nearest way. Thou wouldst be great,
Art not without ambition, but without

The illness should attend it. What thou wouldst highly,
That wouldst thou holily; wouldst not play false,
And yet wouldst wrongly win. Thou'dst have, great Glamis,
That which cries 'Thus thou must do' if thou have it,
And that which rather thou dost fear to do
Than wishest should be undone. Hie thee hither,
That I may pour my spirits in thine ear
And chastise with the valour of my tongue
All that impedes thee from the golden round
Which fate and metaphysical aid doth seem
To have thee crowned withal.

Enter a Servant

What is your tidings?

SERVANT

The King comes here tonight.

LADY MACBETH

Thou'rt mad to say it.
Is not thy master with him, who, were't so,
Would have informed for preparation?

SERVANT

So please you, it is true. Our thane is coming,
One of my fellows had the speed of him,
Who, almost dead for breath, had scarcely more
Than would make up his message.

LADY MACBETH

Give him tending.
He brings great news. *Exit Servant*
The raven himself is hoarse
That croaks the fatal entrance of Duncan
Under my battlements. Come, you spirits
That tend on mortal thoughts, unsex me here,
And fill me from the crown to the toe top-full
Of direst cruelty. Make thick my blood,

Stop up th'access and passage to remorse,
That no compunctious visitings of nature
Shake my fell purpose, nor keep peace between
Th'effect and it. Come to my woman's breasts,
And take my milk for gall, you murd'ring ministers,
Wherever in your sightless substances
You wait on nature's mischief. Come, thick night,
And pall thee in the dunnest smoke of hell,
That my keen knife see not the wound it makes,
Nor heaven peep through the blanket of the dark
To cry 'Hold, hold!'

Enter Macbeth

Great Glamis, worthy Cawdor,
Greater than both by the all-hail hereafter,
Thy letters have transported me beyond
This ignorant present, and I feel now
The future in the instant.

MACBETH My dearest love,
Duncan comes here tonight.

LADY MACBETH And when goes hence?

MACBETH Tomorrow, as he purposes.

LADY MACBETH O never
Shall sun that morrow see.
Your face, my thane, is as a book where men
May read strange matters. To beguile the time,
Look like the time; bear welcome in your eye,
Your hand, your tongue; look like the innocent flower,
But be the serpent under't. He that's coming
Must be provided for; and you shall put
This night's great business into my dispatch,
Which shall to all our nights and days to come

Give solely sovereign sway and masterdom.

MACBETH

We will speak further.

LADY MACBETH Only look up clear.

To alter favour ever is to fear.

Leave all the rest to me. *Exeunt*

Cheryl Campbell played Lady Macbeth with the Royal Shakespeare Company in 1993.

TONY CHURCH

✡

Hamlet

Act I Scene 3

Polonius offers advice to his son, Laertes, who is about to leave Denmark for France.

Yet here, Laertes? Aboard, aboard, for shame!
The wind sits in the shoulder of your sail,
And you are stayed for. There—my blessing with thee,
And these few precepts in thy memory
See thou character. Give thy thoughts no tongue,
Nor any unproportioned thought his act.
Be thou familiar but by no means vulgar.
The friends thou hast, and their adoption tried,
Grapple them to thy soul with hoops of steel,
But do not dull thy palm with entertainment
Of each new-hatched unfledged comrade. Beware
Of entrance to a quarrel, but being in,
Bear't that th'opposèd may beware of thee.
Give every man thine ear but few thy voice.
Take each man's censure, but reserve thy judgement.
Costly thy habit as thy purse can buy,
But not expressed in fancy; rich not gaudy;
For the apparel oft proclaims the man,

And they in France of the best rank and station
Are of all most select and generous chief in that.
Neither a borrower nor a lender be,
For loan oft loses both itself and friend,
And borrowing dulls the edge of husbandry.
This above all—to thine own self be true,
And it must follow, as the night the day,
Thou canst not then be false to any man.
Farewell—my blessing season this in thee.

LAERTES
Most humbly do I take my leave, my lord.

POLONIUS
The time invites you. Go; your servants tend.

LAERTES
Farewell, Ophelia, and remember well
What I have said to you.

OPHELIA 'Tis in my memory locked,
And you yourself shall keep the key of it.

LAERTES
Farewell. *Exit*

POLONIUS
What is't, Ophelia, he hath said to you?

OPHELIA
So please you, something touching the Lord Hamlet.

POLONIUS
Marry, well bethought.
'Tis told me he hath very oft of late
Given private time to you, and you yourself
Have of your audience been most free and bounteous.
If it be so—as so 'tis put on me,
And that in way of caution—I must tell you

You do not understand yourself so clearly
As it behoves my daughter and your honour.
What is between you? Give me up the truth.

OPHELIA

He hath, my lord, of late made many tenders
Of his affection to me.

POLONIUS

Affection, pooh! You speak like a green girl
Unsifted in such perilous circumstance.
Do you believe his 'tenders' as you call them?

OPHELIA

I do not know, my lord, what I should think.

POLONIUS

Marry, I'll teach you: think yourself a baby
That you have ta'en his tenders for true pay,
Which are not sterling. Tender yourself more dearly,
Or—not to crack the wind of the poor phrase,
Running it thus—you'll tender me a fool.

OPHELIA

My lord, he hath importuned me with love
In honourable fashion—

POLONIUS

Ay, fashion you may call it. Go to, go to.

OPHELIA

And hath given countenance to his speech, my lord,
With all the vows of heaven.

POLONIUS

Ay, springes to catch woodcocks. I do know
When the blood burns how prodigal the soul
Lends the tongue vows. These blazes, daughter,
Giving more light than heat, extinct in both

Even in their promise as it is a-making,
You must not take for fire. From this time, daughter,
Be somewhat scanter of your maiden presence.
Set your entreatments at a higher rate
Than a command to parley. For Lord Hamlet,
Believe so much in him, that he is young,
And with a larger tether may he walk
Than may be given you. In few, Ophelia,
Do not believe his vows, for they are brokers,
Not of the dye which their investments show,
But mere imploratators of unholy suits,
Breathing like sanctified and pious bawds
The better to beguile. This is for all—
I would not, in plain terms, from this time forth
Have you so slander any moment leisure
As to give words or talk with the Lord Hamlet.
Look to't, I charge you. Come your ways.

OPHELIA

I shall obey, my lord. *Exeunt*

Tony Church played Polonius with the Royal Shakespeare Company in 1965 and 1980.

BRIAN COX

✡

Titus Andronicus

Act III Scene 1

Titus, whose daughter, Lavinia, has been raped and mutilated, has been tricked into allowing the villainous Aaron to cut off his hand in the expectation that this will cause the Emperor to spare his sons' lives.

TITUS

If there were reason for these miseries,
Then into limits could I bind my woes.
When heaven doth weep, doth not the earth o'erflow?
If the winds rage, doth not the sea wax mad,
Threat'ning the welkin with his big-swoll'n face?
And wilt thou have a reason for this coil?
I am the sea. Hark how her sighs doth blow.
She is the weeping welkin, I the earth.
Then must my sea be movèd with her sighs,
Then must my earth with her continual tears
Become a deluge overflowed and drowned,
Forwhy my bowels cannot hide her woes,
But like a drunkard must I vomit them.
Then give me leave, for losers will have leave
To ease their stomachs with their bitter tongues.

Enter a Messenger with two heads and a hand

MESSENGER

Worthy Andronicus, ill art thou repaid
For that good hand thou sent'st the Emperor.
Here are the heads of thy two noble sons,
And here's thy hand in scorn to thee sent back—
Thy grief their sports, thy resolution mocked,
That woe is me to think upon thy woes
More than remembrance of my father's death.

He sets down the heads and hand. *Exit*

MARCUS

Now let hot Etna cool in Sicily,
And be my heart an ever-burning hell.
These miseries are more than may be borne.
To weep with them that weep doth ease some deal,
But sorrow flouted at is double death.

LUCIUS

Ah, that this sight should make so deep a wound
And yet detested life not shrink thereat—
That ever death should let life bear his name
Where life hath no more interest but to breathe!

Lavinia kisses Titus

MARCUS

Alas, poor heart, that kiss is comfortless
As frozen water to a starvèd snake.

TITUS

When will this fearful slumber have an end?

MARCUS

Now farewell, flatt'ry; die, Andronicus.
Thou dost not slumber. See thy two sons' heads,
Thy warlike hand, thy mangled daughter here,
Thy other banished son with this dear sight

Struck pale and bloodless, and thy brother, I,
Even like a stony image, cold and numb.
Ah, now no more will I control thy griefs.
Rend off thy silver hair, thy other hand
Gnawing with thy teeth, and be this dismal sight
The closing up of our most wretched eyes.
Now is a time to storm. Why art thou still?

TITUS

Ha, ha, ha!

MARCUS

Why dost thou laugh? It fits not with this hour.

TITUS

Why, I have not another tear to shed.
Besides, this sorrow is an enemy,
And would usurp upon my wat'ry eyes
And make them blind with tributary tears.
Then which way shall I find Revenge's cave?—
For these two heads do seem to speak to me
And threat me I shall never come to bliss
Till all these mischiefs be returned again
Even in their throats that hath committed them.
Come, let me see what task I have to do.

He and Lavinia rise

You heavy people, circle me about,
That I may turn me to each one of you
And swear unto my soul to right your wrongs.

Marcus, Lucius, and Lavinia circle Titus. He pledges them

The vow is made. Come, brother, take a head,
And in this hand the other will I bear.
And Lavinia, thou shalt be employed.
Bear thou my hand, sweet wench, between thine arms.

As for thee, boy, go get thee from my sight.
Thou art an exile and thou must not stay.
Hie to the Goths, and raise an army there,
And if ye love me, as I think you do,
Let's kiss and part, for we have much to do.

They kiss. *Exeunt all but Lucius*

LUCIUS

Farewell, Andronicus, my noble father,
The woefull'st man that ever lived in Rome.
Farewell, proud Rome, till Lucius come again;
He loves his pledges dearer than his life.
Farewell, Lavinia, my noble sister:
O, would thou wert as thou tofore hast been!
But now nor Lucius nor Lavinia lives
But in oblivion and hateful griefs.
If Lucius live he will requite your wrongs
And make proud Saturnine and his empress
Beg at the gates like Tarquin and his queen.
Now will I to the Goths and raise a power,
To be revenged on Rome and Saturnine.

Exit

Brian Cox played Titus with the Royal Shakespeare Company in 1987.

NIAḾH CUSACK

✡

As You Like It

Act IV Scene 1

Rosalind, disguised as Ganymede, keeps tryst with Orlando, who is rehearsing his wooing of Rosalind by pretending to believe that 'Ganymede' is Rosalind; Rosalind, in love with Orlando, joins in the pretence. They are joined by Rosalind's cousin Celia, who has taken the name of Aliena

ROSALIND Why, how now, Orlando? Where have you been all this while? You a lover? An you serve me such another trick, never come in my sight more.

ORLANDO My fair Rosalind, I come within an hour of my promise.

ROSALIND Break an hour's promise in love! He that will divide a minute into a thousand parts and break but a part of the thousand part of a minute in the affairs of love, it may be said of him that Cupid hath clapped him o'th' shoulder, but I'll warrant him heartwhole.

ORLANDO Pardon me, dear Rosalind.

ROSALIND Nay, an you be so tardy, come no more in my sight. I had as lief be wooed of a snail.

ORLANDO Of a snail?

ROSALIND Ay, of a snail; for though he comes slowly, he carries his house on his head—a better jointure, I think, than you make a woman. Besides, he brings his destiny with him.

ORLANDO What's that?

ROSALIND Why, horns, which such as you are fain to be beholden to your wives for. But he comes armed in his fortune, and prevents the slander of his wife.

ORLANDO Virtue is no hornmaker, and my Rosalind is virtuous.

ROSALIND And I am your Rosalind.

CELIA It pleases him to call you so; but he hath a Rosalind of a better leer than you.

ROSALIND Come, woo me, woo me, for now I am in a holiday humour, and like enough to consent. What would you say to me now an I were your very, very Rosalind?

ORLANDO I would kiss before I spoke.

ROSALIND Nay, you were better speak first, and when you were gravelled for lack of matter you might take occasion to kiss. Very good orators, when they are out, they will spit; and for lovers, lacking—God warr'nt us—matter, the cleanliest shift is to kiss.

ORLANDO How if the kiss be denied?

ROSALIND Then she puts you to entreaty, and there begins new matter.

ORLANDO Who could be out, being before his belove mistress?

ROSALIND Marry, that should you if I were your mistress, or I should think my honesty ranker than my wit.

ORLANDO What, of my suit?

ROSALIND Not out of your apparel, and yet out of your suit. Am not I your Rosalind?

ORLANDO I take some joy to say you are because I would be talking of her.

ROSALIND Well, in her person I say I will not have you.

ORLANDO Then in mine own person I die.

ROSALIND No, faith; die by attorney. The poor world is almost six thousand years old, and in all this time there was not any man died in his own person, videlicet, in a love-cause. Troilus had his brains dashed out with a Grecian club, yet he did what he could to die before, and he is one of the patterns of love. Leander, he would have lived many a fair year though Hero had turned nun if it had not been for a hot midsummer night, for, good youth, he went but forth to wash him in the Hellespont and, being taken with the cramp, was drowned; and the foolish chroniclers of that age found it was Hero of Sestos. But these are all lies. Men have died from time to time, and worms have eaten them, but not for love.

ORLANDO I would not have my right Rosalind of this mind, for I protest her frown might kill me.

ROSALIND By this hand, it will not kill a fly. But come, now I will be your Rosalind in a more coming-on disposition; and ask me what you will, I will grant it.

ORLANDO Then love me, Rosalind.

ROSALIND Yes, faith, will I, Fridays and Saturdays and all.

ORLANDO And wilt thou have me?

ROSALIND Ay, and twenty such.

ORLANDO What sayst thou?

ROSALIND Are you not good?

ORLANDO I hope so.

ROSALIND Why then, can one desire too much of a good thing? (*To Celia*) Come, sister, you shall be the priest and marry us.—Give me your hand, Orlando.—What do you say, sister?

ORLANDO (*to Celia*) Pray thee, marry us.

CELIA I cannot say the words.

ROSALIND You must begin, 'Will you, Orlando'—

CELIA Go to. Will you, Orlando, have to wife this Rosalind?

ORLANDO I will.

ROSALIND Ay, but when?

ORLANDO Why now, as fast as she can marry us.

ROSALIND Then you must say, 'I take thee, Rosalind, for wife.'

ORLANDO I take thee, Rosalind, for wife.

ROSALIND I might ask you for your commission; but I do take thee, Orlando, for my husband. There's a girl goes before the priest; and certainly a woman's thought runs before her actions.

ORLANDO So do all thoughts; they are winged.

ROSALIND Now tell me how long you would have her after you have possessed her?

ORLANDO For ever and a day.

ROSALIND Say a day without the ever. No, no, Orlando; men are April when they woo, December when they wed. Maids are May when they are maids, but the sky changes when they are wives. I will be more jealous of thee than a Barbary cock-pigeon over his hen, more clamorous than a parrot against rain, more new-fangled than an ape, more giddy in my desires than a monkey. I will weep for nothing, like Diana in the fountain, and I will do that when you are disposed to be merry. I will laugh like a hyena, and that when thou art inclined to sleep.

ORLANDO But will my Rosalind do so?

ROSALIND By my life, she will do as I do.

ORLANDO O, but she is wise.

ROSALIND Or else she could not have the wit to do this. The

wiser, the waywarder. Make the doors upon a woman's wit, and it will out at the casement. Shut that, and 'twill out at the key-hole. Stop that, 'twill fly with the smoke out at the chimney.

ORLANDO A man that had a wife with such a wit, he might say 'Wit, whither wilt?'

ROSALIND Nay, you might keep that check for it till you met your wife's wit going to your neighbour's bed.

ORLANDO And what wit could wit have to excuse that?

ROSALIND Marry, to say she came to seek you there. You shall never take her without her answer unless you take her without her tongue. O, that woman that cannot make her fault her husband's occasion, let her never nurse her child herself, for she will breed it like a fool.

ORLANDO For these two hours, Rosalind, I will leave thee.

ROSALIND Alas, dear love, I cannot lack thee two hours.

ORLANDO I must attend the Duke at dinner. By two o'clock I will be with thee again.

ROSALIND Ay, go your ways, go your ways. I knew what you would prove; my friends told me as much, and I thought no less. That flattering tongue of yours won me. 'Tis but one cast away, and so, come, death! Two o'clock is your hour?

ORLANDO Ay, sweet Rosalind.

ROSALIND By my troth, and in good earnest, and so God mend me, and by all pretty oaths that are not dangerous, if you break one jot of your promise or come one minute behind your hour, I will think you the most pathetical break-promise, and the most hollow lover, and the most unworthy of her you call Rosalind that may be chosen out of the gross band of the unfaithful. Therefore beware my censure, and keep your promise.

ORLANDO With no less religion than if thou wert indeed my Rosalind. So, adieu.

ROSALIND Well, Time is the old justice that examines all such offenders; and let Time try. Adieu.

Exit Orlando

CELIA You have simply misused our sex in your love-prate. We must have your doublet and hose plucked over your head, and show the world what the bird hath done to her own nest.

ROSALIND O coz, coz, coz, my pretty little coz, that thou didst know how many fathom deep I am in love. But it cannot be sounded. My affection hath an unknown bottom, like the Bay of Portugal.

CELIA Or rather bottomless, that as fast as you pour affection in, it runs out.

ROSALIND No, that same wicked bastard of Venus, that was begot of thought, conceived of spleen, and born of madness, that blind rascally boy that abuses everyone's eyes because his own are out, let him be judge how deep I am in love. I'll tell thee, Aliena, I cannot be out of the sight of Orlando. I'll go find a shadow and sigh till he come.

CELIA And I'll sleep.

Niaḿh Cusack played Rosalind with the Royal Shakespeare Company in 1996.

SINEAD CUSACK

✡

Much Ado About Nothing

Act IV Scene 1

The young soldier Claudio, tricked into believing that his fiancée Hero has a lover, has rejected her at the altar.

BENEDICK Lady Beatrice, have you wept all this while?
BEATRICE Yea, and I will weep a while longer.
BENEDICK I will not desire that.
BEATRICE You have no reason, I do it freely.
BENEDICK Surely I do believe your fair cousin is wronged.
BEATRICE Ah, how much might the man deserve of me that would right her!
BENEDICK Is there any way to show such friendship?
BEATRICE A very even way, but no such friend.
BENEDICK May a man do it?
BEATRICE It is a man's office, but not yours.
BENEDICK I do love nothing in the world so well as you. Is not that strange?
BEATRICE As strange as the thing I know not. It were as possible for me to say I loved nothing so well as you, but believe me not, and yet I lie not. I confess nothing nor I deny nothing. I am sorry for my cousin.
BENEDICK By my sword, Beatrice, thou lovest me.
BEATRICE Do not swear and eat it.

BENEDICK I will swear by it that you love me, and I will make him eat it that says I love not you.

BEATRICE Will you not eat your word?

BENEDICK With no sauce that can be devised to it. I protest I love thee.

BEATRICE Why then, God forgive me.

BENEDICK What offence, sweet Beatrice?

BEATRICE You have stayed me in a happy hour. I was about to protest I loved you.

BENEDICK And do it with all thy heart.

BEATRICE I love you with so much of my heart that none is left to protest.

BENEDICK Come, bid me do anything for thee.

BEATRICE Kill Claudio.

BENEDICK Ha! Not for the wide world.

BEATRICE You kill me to deny it. Farewell.

BENEDICK Tarry, sweet Beatrice.

BEATRICE I am gone though I am here. There is no love in you.—Nay, I pray you, let me go.

BENEDICK Beatrice.

BEATRICE In faith, I will go.

BENEDICK We'll be friends first.

BEATRICE You dare easier be friends with me than fight with mine enemy.

BENEDICK Is Claudio thine enemy?

BEATRICE Is a not approved in the height a villain, that hath slandered, scorned, dishonoured my kinswoman? O that I were a man! What, bear her in hand until they come to take hands, and then with public accusation, uncovered slander, unmitigated rancour—O God that I were a man! I would eat his heart in the market place.

BENEDICK Hear me, Beatrice.

BEATRICE Talk with a man out at a window—a proper saying!

BENEDICK Nay, but Beatrice.

BEATRICE Sweet Hero, she is wronged, she is slandered, she is undone.

BENEDICK Beat—

BEATRICE Princes and counties! Surely a princely testimony, a goodly count, Count Comfit, a sweet gallant, surely. O that I were a man for his sake! Or that I had any friend would be a man for my sake! But manhood is melted into courtesies, valour into compliment, and men are only turned into tongue, and trim ones, too. He is now as valiant as Hercules that only tells a lie and swears it. I cannot be a man with wishing, therefore I will die a woman with grieving.

BENEDICK Tarry, good Beatrice. By this hand, I love thee.

BEATRICE Use it for my love some other way than swearing by it.

BENEDICK Think you in your soul the Count Claudio hath wronged Hero?

BEATRICE Yea, as sure as I have a thought or a soul.

BENEDICK Enough, I am engaged, I will challenge him. I will kiss your hand, and so I leave you. By this hand, Claudio shall render me a dear account. As you hear of me, so think of me. Go comfort your cousin. I must say she is dead. And so, farewell.

Sinead Cusack played Beatrice with the Royal Shakespeare Company in 1982.

JUDI DENCH

☆

Antony and Cleopatra

Act V, Scene 2

Mark Antony, tricked by Cleopatra into believing that she has killed herself, has himself committed suicide.

DOLABELLA
Most noble Empress, you have heard of me.
CLEOPATRA
I cannot tell
DOLABELLA Assurèdly you know me.
CLEOPATRA
No matter, sir, what I have heard or known.
You laugh when boys or women tell their dreams;
Is't not your trick?
DOLABELLA I understand not, madam.
CLEOPATRA
I dreamt there was an Emperor Antony.
O, such another sleep, that I might see
But such another man!
DOLABELLA If it might please ye—
CLEOPATRA
His face was as the heav'ns, and therein stuck
A sun and moon, which kept their course and lighted
The little O o'th' earth.

DOLABELLA Most sovereign creature—

CLEOPATRA

His legs bestrid the ocean; his reared arm
Crested the world. His voice was propertied
As all the tunèd spheres, and that to friends;
But when he meant to quail and shake the orb,
He was as rattling thunder. For his bounty,
There was no winter in't; an autumn 'twas,
That grew the more by reaping. His delights
Were dolphin-like; they showed his back above
The element they lived in. In his livery
Walked crowns and crownets. Realms and islands were
As plates dropped from his pocket.

DOLABELLA Cleopatra—

CLEOPATRA

Think you there was, or might be, such a man
As this I dreamt of?

DOLABELLA Gentle madam, no.

CLEOPATRA

You lie, up to the hearing of the gods.
But if there be, or ever were one such,
It's past the size of dreaming. Nature wants stuff
To vie strange forms with fancy; yet t'imagine
An Antony were nature's piece 'gainst fancy,
Condemning shadows quite.

DOLABELLA Hear me, good madam:

Your loss is as yourself, great, and you bear it
As answering to the weight. Would I might never
O'ertake pursued success but I do feel,
By the rebound of yours, a grief that smites
My very heart at root.

CLEOPATRA I thank you, sir.
Know you what Caesar means to do with me?

DOLABELLA
I am loath to tell you what I would you knew.

CLEOPATRA
Nay, pray you, sir.

DOLABELLA Though he be honourable—

CLEOPATRA
He'll lead me then in triumph.

DOLABELLA Madam, he will, I know't.

Judi Dench, whose many roles with the Royal Shakespeare Company include Isabella, Lady Macbeth, Viola, and Beatrice, played Cleopatra in 1987, for the Royal National Theatre.

RALPH FIENNES

✡

Hamlet

Act III Scene 2

Hamlet speaks to the Players who have come to visit the Danish court.

Speak the speech, I pray you, as I pronounced it to you—trippingly on the tongue; but if you mouth it, as many of your players do, I had as lief the town-crier had spoke my lines. Nor do not saw the air too much with your hand, thus, but use all gently; for in the very torrent, tempest, and as I may say the whirlwind of your passion, you must acquire and beget a temperance that may give it smoothness. O, it offends me to the soul to hear a robustious, periwig-pated fellow tear a passion to tatters, to very rags, to split the ears of the groundlings, who for the most part are capable of nothing but inexplicable dumb shows and noise. I would have such a fellow whipped for o'erdoing Termagant. It out-Herods Herod. Pray you avoid it.

A PLAYER I warrant your honour.

HAMLET Be not too tame, neither; but let your own discretion be your tutor. Suit the action to the word, the word to the action, with this special observance: that you o'erstep not the modesty of nature. For anything so overdone is from the purpose of playing, whose end, both at the first and now, was and is to hold as 'twere the mirror up to nature, to show virtue her own feature, scorn her own image, and the very age and body of the time his form and pressure. Now this overdone, or come tardy off, though it make the unskilful laugh, cannot but make the judicious grieve; the censure of the which one must in your allowance o'erweigh a whole theatre of others. O, there be players that I have seen play, and heard others praise, and that highly, not to speak it profanely, that neither having the accent of Christians nor the gait of Christian, pagan, nor no man, have so strutted and bellowed that I have thought some of nature's journeymen had made men, and not made them well, they imitated humanity so abominably.

A PLAYER I hope we have reformed that indifferently with us, sir.

HAMLET O, reform it altogether. And let those that play your clowns speak no more than is set down for them; for there be of them that will themselves laugh to set on some quantity of barren spectators to laugh too, though in the mean time some necessary question of the play be then to be considered. That's villainous, and shows a most pitiful ambition in the fool that uses it. Go make you ready.

Ralph Fiennes's roles with the Royal Shakespeare Company include Henry VI and Troilus. He played Hamlet in 1995 with the Almeida Theatre Company.

MICHAEL GAMBON

✡

King Lear

Act II Scene 2

Lear, having shared his kingdom between his daughters Goneril and Regan, finds that they are not willing to abide by the conditions he seeks to impose on them.

LEAR

I prithee, daughter, do not make me mad.
I will not trouble thee, my child. Farewell.
We'll no more meet, no more see one another.
But yet thou art my flesh, my blood, my daughter—
Or rather a disease that's in my flesh,
Which I must needs call mine. Thou art a boil,
A plague-sore or embossèd carbuncle
In my corrupted blood. But I'll not chide thee.
Let shame come when it will, I do not call it.
I do not bid the thunder-bearer shoot,
Nor tell tales of thee to high-judging Jove.
Mend when thou canst; be better at thy leisure.
I can be patient, I can stay with Regan,
I and my hundred knights.

REGAN Not altogether so.

I looked not for you yet, nor am provided

For your fit welcome. Give ear, sir, to my sister;
For those that mingle reason with your passion
Must be content to think you old, and so—
But she knows what she does.

LEAR
Is this well spoken?

REGAN
I dare avouch it, sir. What, fifty followers?
Is it not well? What should you need of more,
Yea, or so many, sith that both charge and danger
Speak 'gainst so great a number? How in one house
Should many people under two commands
Hold amity? 'Tis hard, almost impossible.

GONERIL
Why might not you, my lord, receive attendance
From those that she calls servants, or from mine?

REGAN
Why not, my lord? If then they chanced to slack ye,
We could control them. If you will come to me—
For now I spy a danger—I entreat you
To bring but five-and-twenty; to no more
Will I give place or notice.

LEAR
I gave you all.

REGAN
And in good time you gave it.

LEAR
Made you my guardians, my depositaries,
But kept a reservation to be followed
With such a number. What, must I come to you
With five-and-twenty? Regan, said you so?

REGAN
And speak't again, my lord. No more with me.

LEAR

Those wicked creatures yet do look well favoured
When others are more wicked. Not being the worst
Stands in some rank of praise. (*To Goneril*) I'll go with thee.
Thy fifty yet doth double five-and-twenty,
And thou art twice her love.

GONERIL Hear me, my lord.
What need you five-and-twenty, ten, or five,
To follow in a house where twice so many
Have a command to tend you?

REGAN What need one?

LEAR

O, reason not the need! Our basest beggars
Are in the poorest thing superfluous.
Allow not nature more than nature needs,
Man's life is cheap as beast's. Thou art a lady.
If only to go warm were gorgeous,
Why, nature needs not what thou, gorgeous, wear'st,
Which scarcely keeps thee warm. But for true need—
You heavens, give me that patience, patience I need.
You see me here, you gods, a poor old man,
As full of grief as age, wretchèd in both.
If it be you that stirs these daughters' hearts
Against their father, fool me not so much
To bear it tamely. Touch me with noble anger,
And let not women's weapons, water-drops,
Stain my man's cheeks. No, you unnatural hags,
I will have such revenges on you both
That all the world shall—I will do such things—
What they are, yet I know not; but they shall be
The terrors of the earth. You think I'll weep.

No, I'll not weep. I have full cause of weeping,
Storm and tempest
But this heart shall break into a hundred thousand flaws
Or ere I'll weep.—O Fool, I shall go mad!
Exeunt Lear, Fool, Gentleman, and Gloucester

Michael Gambon played Lear with the Royal Shakespeare Company in 1982.

JOHN GIELGUD

☆

Henry IV, Part Two

Act III, Scene 2

Justice Shallow reminiscences with his cousin Justice Silence in his Gloucestershire home before welcoming Sir John Falstaff, who has come to recruit soldiers.

SHALLOW Come on, come on, come on! Give me your hand, sir, give me your hand, sir. An early stirrer, by the rood! And how doth my good cousin Silence?

SILENCE Good morrow, good cousin Shallow.

SHALLOW And how doth my cousin your bedfellow? And your fairest daughter and mine, my god-daughter Ellen?

SILENCE Alas, a black ouzel, cousin Shallow.

SHALLOW By yea and no, sir, I dare say my cousin William is become a good scholar. He is at Oxford still, is he not?

SILENCE Indeed, sir, to my cost.

SHALLOW A must then to the Inns o' Court shortly. I was once of Clement's Inn, where I think they will talk of mad Shallow yet.

SILENCE You were called 'lusty Shallow' then, cousin.

SHALLOW By the mass, I was called anything; and I would have done anything indeed, too, and roundly, too. There was I, and little John Doit of Staffordshire, and black George

Barnes, and Francis Pickbone, and Will Squeal, a Cotswold man; you had not four such swinge-bucklers in all the Inns o' Court again. And I may say to you, we knew where the bona-robas were, and had the best of them all at commandment. Then was Jack Falstaff, now Sir John, a boy, and page to Thomas Mowbray, Duke of Norfolk.

SILENCE This Sir John, cousin, that comes hither anon about soldiers?

SHALLOW The same Sir John, the very same. I see him break Scoggin's head at the court gate when a was a crack, not thus high. And the very same day did I fight with one Samson Stockfish, a fruiterer, behind Gray's Inn. Jesu, Jesu, the mad days that I have spent! And to see how many of my old acquaintance are dead.

SILENCE We shall all follow, cousin.

SHALLOW Certain, 'tis certain; very sure, very sure. Death, as the Psalmist saith, is certain to all; all shall die. How a good yoke of bullocks at Stamford fair?

SILENCE By my troth, I was not there.

SHALLOW Death is certain. Is old Double of your town living yet?

SILENCE Dead, sir.

SHALLOW Jesu, Jesu, dead! A drew a good bow; and dead! A shot a fine shoot. John o' Gaunt loved him well, and betted much money on his head. Dead! A would have clapped i'th' clout at twelve score, and carried you a forehand shaft a fourteen and fourteen and a half, that it would have done a man's heart good to see. How a score of ewes now?

SILENCE Thereafter as they be. A score of good ewes may be worth ten pounds.

SHALLOW And is old Double dead?

Later, they continue their reminiscences with Falstaff

SHALLOW O, Sir John, do you remember since we lay all night in the Windmill in Saint George's Field?

SIR JOHN No more of that, good Master Shallow, no more of that.

SHALLOW Ha, 'twas a merry night! And is Jane Nightwork alive?

SIR JOHN She lives, Master Shallow.

SHALLOW She never could away with me.

SIR JOHN Never, never. She would always say she could not abide Master Shallow.

SHALLOW By the mass, I could anger her to th' heart. She was then a bona-roba. Doth she hold her own well?

SIR JOHN Old, old, Master Shallow.

SHALLOW Nay, she must be old; she cannot choose but be old; certain she's old; and had Robin Nightwork by old Nightwork before I came to Clement's Inn.

SILENCE That's fifty-five year ago.

SHALLOW Ha, cousin Silence, that thou hadst seen that that this knight and I have seen! Ha, Sir John, said I well?

SIR JOHN We have heard the chimes at midnight, Master Shallow.

King Lear

Act IV Scene 4

Lear, who had rejected his youngest daughter, Cordelia, is reunited with her after great suffering

CORDELIA
How does my royal lord? How fares your majesty?
LEAR
You do me wrong to take me out o'th' grave.
Thou art a soul in bliss, but I am bound
Upon a wheel of fire, that mine own tears
Do scald like molten lead.
CORDELIA Sir, do you know me?
LEAR
You are a spirit, I know. Where did you die?
CORDELIA (*to the Gentleman*) Still, still far wide!
FIRST GENTLEMAN
He's scarce awake. Let him alone a while.
LEAR
Where have I been? Where am I? Fair daylight?
I am mightily abused. I should ev'n die with pity
To see another thus. I know not what to say.
I will not swear these are my hands. Let's see:
I feel this pin prick. Would I were assured
Of my condition.
CORDELIA (*kneeling*) O look upon me, sir,
And hold your hands in benediction o'er me.
You must not kneel.

LEAR Pray do not mock.
I am a very foolish, fond old man,
Fourscore and upward,
Not an hour more nor less; and to deal plainly,
I fear I am not in my perfect mind.
Methinks I should know you, and know this man;
Yet I am doubtful, for I am mainly ignorant
What place this is; and all the skill I have
Remembers not these garments; nor I know not
Where I did lodge last night. Do not laugh at me,
For as I am a man, I think this lady
To be my child, Cordelia.

CORDELIA And so I am, I am.

LEAR
Be your tears wet? Yes, faith. I pray, weep not.
If you have poison for me, I will drink it.
I know you do not love me; for your sisters
Have, as I do remember, done me wrong.
You have some cause; they have not.

CORDELIA No cause, no cause.

LEAR
Am I in France?

KENT
In your own kingdom, sir.

LEAR
Do not abuse me.

FIRST GENTLEMAN
Be comforted, good madam. The great rage
You see is killed in him. Desire him to go in.
Trouble him no more till further settling.

CORDELIA (*to Lear*) Will't please your highness walk?

LEAR

You must bear with me. Pray you now, forget
And forgive. I am old and foolish.

Exeunt

Sir John Gielgud played Justice Shallow in a recital programme at the Royal Shakespeare Theatre in 1981. He played King Lear at Stratford-upon-Avon in 1955.

JULIAN GLOVER

✡

Henry IV, Part One

Act I, Scene 1

At the opening of the play King Henry, who has usurped the throne of Richard II, expresses his intention to make a pilgrimage to the Holy Land.

So shaken as we are, so wan with care,
Find we a time for frighted peace to pant
And breathe short-winded accents of new broils
To be commenced in strands afar remote.
No more the thirsty entrance of this soil
Shall daub her lips with her own children's blood.
No more shall trenching war channel her fields,
Nor bruise her flow'rets with the armèd hoofs
Of hostile paces. Those opposèd eyes,
Which, like the meteors of a troubled heaven,
All of one nature, of one substance bred,
Did lately meet in the intestine shock
And furious close of civil butchery,
Shall now in mutual well-beseeming ranks
March all one way, and be no more opposed
Against acquaintance, kindred, and allies.
The edge of war, like an ill-sheathèd knife,

No more shall cut his master. Therefore, friends,
As far as to the sepulchre of Christ—
Whose soldier now, under whose blessèd cross
We are impressèd and engaged to fight—
Forthwith a power of English shall we levy,
Whose arms were moulded in their mothers' womb
To chase these pagans in those holy fields
Over whose acres walked those blessèd feet
Which fourteen hundred years ago were nailed,
For our advantage, on the bitter cross.
But this our purpose now is twelve month old,
And bootless 'tis to tell you we will go.

Romeo and Juliet

Act II, Scene 2

Friar Laurence, embarking on his morning task of gathering herbs, reflects on their various properties.

The grey-eyed morn smiles on the frowning night,
Chequ'ring the eastern clouds with streaks of light,
And fleckled darkness like a drunkard reels
From forth day's path and Titan's fiery wheels.
Now, ere the sun advance his burning eye
The day to cheer and night's dank dew to dry,
I must up-fill this osier cage of ours
With baleful weeds and precious-juicèd flowers.
The earth, that's nature's mother, is her tomb.

What is her burying grave, that is her womb,
And from her womb children of divers kind
We sucking on her natural bosom find,
Many for many virtues excellent,
None but for some, and yet all different.
O mickle is the powerful grace that lies
In plants, herbs, stones, and their true qualities,
For naught so vile that on the earth doth live
But to the earth some special good doth give;
Nor aught so good but, strained from that fair use,
Revolts from true birth, stumbling on abuse.
Virtue itself turns vice being misapplied,
And vice sometime's by action dignified.
Enter Romeo
Within the infant rind of this weak flower
Poison hath residence, and medicine power,
For this, being smelt, with that part cheers each part;
Being tasted, slays all senses with the heart.
Two such opposèd kings encamp them still
In man as well as herbs—grace and rude will;
And where the worser is predominant,
Full soon the canker death eats up that plant.

Julian Glover played King Henry with the Royal Shakespeare Company in 1991, and Friar Laurence in 1995.

RICHARD GRIFFITHS

✲

Julius Caesar

Act I Scene 1

Marullus, a tribune, berates the Roman citizens for celebrating Caesar's triumph.

Wherefore rejoice? What conquest brings he home?
What tributaries follow him to Rome
To grace in captive bonds his chariot wheels?
You blocks, you stones, you worse than senseless things!
O, you hard hearts, you cruel men of Rome,
Knew you not Pompey? Many a time and oft
Have you climbed up to walls and battlements,
To towers and windows, yea to chimney-tops,
Your infants in your arms, and there have sat
The livelong day with patient expectation
To see great Pompey pass the streets of Rome.
And when you saw his chariot but appear,
Have you not made an universal shout,
That Tiber trembled underneath her banks
To hear the replication of your sounds
Made in her concave shores?
And do you now put on your best attire?
And do you now cull out a holiday?

And do you now strew flowers in his way
That comes in triumph over Pompey's blood?
Be gone!
Run to your houses, fall upon your knees,
Pray to the gods to intermit the plague
That needs must light on this ingratitude.

Love's Labour's Lost

Act I Scene 1

At the play's opening, Ferdinand, King of Navarre, urges his friends to subscribe to an agreement to withdraw from the world's temptations for a period of three years' study.

KING

Let fame, that all hunt after in their lives,
Live registered upon our brazen tombs,
And then grace us in the disgrace of death
When, spite of cormorant devouring time,
Th'endeavour of this present breath may buy
That honour which shall bate his scythe's keen edge
And make us heirs of all eternity.
Therefore, brave conquerors—for so you are,
That war against your own affections
And the huge army of the world's desires—
Our late edict shall strongly stand in force.
Navarre shall be the wonder of the world.
Our court shall be a little academe,

Still and contemplative in living art.
You three—Berowne, Dumaine, and Longueville—
Have sworn for three years' term to live with me
My fellow scholars, and to keep those statutes
That are recorded in this schedule here.
Your oaths are passed; and now subscribe your names,
That his own hand may strike his honour down
That violates the smallest branch herein.
If you are armed to do as sworn to do,
Subscribe to your deep oaths, and keep it, too.

Henry VIII (All is True)

Prologue

I come no more to make you laugh. Things now
That bear a weighty and a serious brow,
Sad, high, and working, full of state and woe—
Such noble scenes as draw the eye to flow
We now present. Those that can pity here
May, if they think it well, let fall a tear.
The subject will deserve it. Such as give
Their money out of hope they may believe,
May here find truth, too. Those that come to see
Only a show or two, and so agree
The play may pass, if they be still, and willing,
I'll undertake may see away their shilling
Richly in two short hours. Only they
That come to hear a merry bawdy play,

A noise of targets, or to see a fellow
In a long motley coat guarded with yellow,
Will be deceived. For, gentle hearers, know
To rank our chosen truth with such a show
As fool and fight is, beside forfeiting
Our own brains, and the opinion that we bring
To make that only true we now intend,
Will leave us never an understanding friend.
Therefore, for goodness' sake, and as you are known
The first and happiest hearers of the town,
Be sad as we would make ye. Think ye see
The very persons of our noble story
As they were living; think you see them great,
And followed with the general throng and sweat
Of thousand friends; then, in a moment, see
How soon this mightiness meets misery.
And if you can be merry then, I'll say
A man may weep upon his wedding day.

Richard Griffiths played the King in *Love's Labour's Lost* with the Royal Shakespeare Company in 1978, and both the Prologue and Henry VIII in 1983.

IAN HOGG

✡

Coriolanus

Act III, Scene 3

Coriolanus, banished from his native Rome 'As enemy to the people and his country', berates his enemies.

You common cry of curs, whose breath I hate
As reek o'th' rotten fens, whose loves I prize
As the dead carcasses of unburied men
That do corrupt my air: I banish you.
And here remain with your uncertainty.
Let every feeble rumour shake your hearts;
Your enemies, with nodding of their plumes,
Fan you into despair! Have the power still
To banish your defenders, till at length
Your ignorance—which finds not till it feels—
Making but reservation of yourselves,
Still your own foes, deliver you
As most abated captives to some nation
That won you without blows! Despising
For you the city, thus I turn my back.
There is a world elsewhere.

King Lear

Act V Scene 3

The captive Lear, reunited with his daughter Cordelia, imagines a future with her in prison

LEAR ... Come, let's away to prison.
We two alone will sing like birds i'th' cage.
When thou dost ask me blessing, I'll kneel down
And ask of thee forgiveness; so we'll live,
And pray, and sing, and tell old tales, and laugh
At gilded butterflies, and hear poor rogues
Talk of court news, and we'll talk with them too—
Who loses and who wins, who's in, who's out,
And take upon 's the mystery of things
As if we were God's spies; and we'll wear out
In a walled prison packs and sects of great ones
That ebb and flow by th' moon.
EDMUND (*to soldiers*) Take them away.
LEAR Upon such sacrifices, my Cordelia,
The gods themselves throw incense. Have I caught thee?
He that parts us shall bring a brand from heaven
And fire us hence like foxes. Wipe thine eyes.
The goodyear shall devour them, flesh and fell,
Ere they shall make us weep. We'll see 'em starved first.
Come.

Ian Hogg played Coriolanus with the Royal Shakespeare Company in 1972.

IAN HOLM

✡

Henry V

Act IV Scene 1

Alone, the King meditates on kingly responsibility.

Upon the King.
'Let us our lives, our souls, our debts, our care-full wives,
Our children, and our sins, lay on the King.'
We must bear all. O hard condition,
Twin-born with greatness: subject to the breath
Of every fool, whose sense no more can feel
But his own wringing. What infinite heartsease
Must kings neglect that private men enjoy?
And what have kings that privates have not too,
Save ceremony, save general ceremony?
And what art thou, thou idol ceremony?
What kind of god art thou, that suffer'st more
Of mortal griefs than do thy worshippers?
What are thy rents? What are thy comings-in?
O ceremony, show me but thy worth.
What is thy soul of adoration?
Art thou aught else but place, degree, and form,
Creating awe and fear in other men?
Wherein thou art less happy, being feared,

Than they in fearing.
What drink'st thou oft, instead of homage sweet,
But poisoned flattery? O be sick, great greatness,
And bid thy ceremony give thee cure.
Think'st thou the fiery fever will go out
With titles blown from adulation?
Will it give place to flexure and low bending?
Canst thou, when thou command'st the beggar's knee,
Command the health of it? No, thou proud dream
That play'st so subtly with a king's repose;
I am a king that find thee, and I know
'Tis not the balm, the sceptre, and the ball,
The sword, the mace, the crown imperial,
The intertissued robe of gold and pearl,
The farcèd title running fore the king,
The throne he sits on, nor the tide of pomp
That beats upon the high shore of this world—
No, not all these, thrice-gorgeous ceremony,
Not all these, laid in bed majestical,
Can sleep so soundly as the wretched slave
Who with a body filled and vacant mind
Gets him to rest, crammed with distressful bread;
Never sees horrid night, the child of hell,
But like a lackey from the rise to set
Sweats in the eye of Phoebus, and all night
Sleeps in Elysium; next day, after dawn
Doth rise and help Hyperion to his horse,
And follows so the ever-running year
With profitable labour to his grave.
And but for ceremony such a wretch,
Winding up days with toil and nights with sleep,

Had the forehand and vantage of a king.
The slave, a member of the country's peace,
Enjoys it, but in gross brain little wots
What watch the King keeps to maintain the peace,
Whose hours the peasant best advantages.

Ian Holm played Henry V with the Royal Shakespeare Company in 1964.

ALAN HOWARD

✡

Henry IV, Part One

Act I Scene 2

Prince Hal, left alone after plotting highway robbery with Falstaff and others, explains himself.

I know you all, and will a while uphold
The unyoked humour of your idleness.
Yet herein will I imitate the sun,
Who doth permit the base contagious clouds
To smother up his beauty from the world,
That when he please again to be himself,
Being wanted he may be more wondered at
By breaking through the foul and ugly mists
Of vapours that did seem to strangle him.
If all the year were playing holidays,
To sport would be as tedious as to work;
But when they seldom come, they wished-for come,
And nothing pleaseth but rare accidents.
So when this loose behaviour I throw off
And pay the debt I never promisèd,
By how much better than my word I am,
By so much shall I falsify men's hopes;
And like bright metal on a sullen ground,

My reformation, glitt'ring o'er my fault,
Shall show more goodly and attract more eyes
Than that which hath no foil to set it off.
I'll so offend to make offence a skill,
Redeeming time when men think least I will.

Alan Howard played Prince Hal with the Royal Shakespeare Company in 1975.

JEREMY IRONS

✡

Richard II

Act V Scene 5

Imprisoned and alone, the King, deposed by Bolingbroke, meditates on his condition.

I have been studying how I may compare
This prison where I live unto the world;
And for because the world is populous,
And here is not a creature but myself,
I cannot do it. Yet I'll hammer it out.
My brain I'll prove the female to my soul,
My soul the father, and these two beget
A generation of still-breeding thoughts;
And these same thoughts people this little world
In humours like the people of this world.
For no thought is contented. The better sort,
As thoughts of things divine, are intermixed
With scruples, and do set the faith itself
Against the faith, as thus: 'Come, little ones',
And then again,
'It is as hard to come as for a camel
To thread the postern of a small needle's eye.'
Thoughts tending to ambition, they do plot

Unlikely wonders: how these vain weak nails
May tear a passage through the flinty ribs
Of this hard world, my ragged prison walls;
And for they cannot, die in their own pride.
Thoughts tending to content flatter themselves
That they are not the first of fortune's slaves,
Nor shall not be the last—like seely beggars,
Who, sitting in the stocks, refuge their shame
That many have, and others must, set there;
And in this thought they find a kind of ease,
Bearing their own misfortunes on the back
Of such as have before endured the like.
Thus play I in one person many people,
And none contented. Sometimes am I king;
Then treason makes me wish myself a beggar,
And so I am. Then crushing penury
Persuades me I was better when a king.
Then am I kinged again, and by and by
Think that I am unkinged by Bolingbroke,
And straight am nothing. But whate'er I be,
Nor I, nor any man that but man is,
With nothing shall be pleased till he be eased
With being nothing.

Music plays

Music do I hear.

Ha, ha; keep time! How sour sweet music is
When time is broke and no proportion kept.
So is it in the music of men's lives.
And here have I the daintiness of ear
To check time broke in a disordered string;
But for the concord of my state and time

Had not an ear to hear my true time broke.
I wasted time, and now doth time waste me,
For now hath time made me his numb'ring clock.
My thoughts are minutes, and with sighs they jar
Their watches on unto mine eyes, the outward watch
Whereto my finger, like a dial's point,
Is pointing still in cleansing them from tears.
Now, sir, the sounds that tell what hour it is
Are clamorous groans that strike upon my heart,
Which is the bell. So sighs, and tears, and groans
Show minutes, hours, and times. But my time
Runs posting on in Bolingbroke's proud joy,
While I stand fooling here, his jack of the clock.
This music mads me. Let it sound no more,
For though it have holp madmen to their wits,
In me it seems it will make wise men mad.

The music ceases

Yet blessing on his heart that gives it me,
For 'tis a sign of love, and love to Richard
Is a strange brooch in this all-hating world.

Enter a Groom of the stable

GROOM Hail, royal Prince!

RICHARD Thanks, noble peer.
The cheapest of us is ten groats too dear.
What art thou, and how com'st thou hither,
Where no man never comes but that sad dog
That brings me food to make misfortune live?

Jeremy Irons played Richard II with the Royal Shakespeare Company in 1986.

DEREK JACOBI

✡

Pericles

Act V Scene 1

Pericles, King of Tyre, believes that his wife, Thaisa, died giving birth to their daughter Marina, whom he believes to have died in childhood. Now, after long travel he is in a comatose state on board ship off Mytilene. Lysimachus, governor of Mytilene, has invited Marina, her identity unknown, to try to bring Pericles to himself.

MARINA   Sir, I will use
  My utmost skill in his recure, provided
  That none but I and my companion maid
  Be suffered to come near him.
LYSIMACHUS (*to the others*)   Come, let us leave her,
  And the gods make her prosperous.
        Marina sings
LYSIMACHUS   Marked he your music?
MAID No, nor looked on us.
LYSIMACHUS   See, she will speak to him.
MARINA (*to Pericles*) Hail, sir; my lord, lend ear.
PERICLES Hmh, ha!
        He pushes her back
MARINA I am a maid,
  My lord, that ne'er before invited eyes,

But have been gazed on like a comet. She speaks,
My lord, that maybe hath endured a grief
Might equal yours, if both were justly weighed.
Though wayward fortune did malign my state,
My derivation was from ancestors
Who stood equivalent with mighty kings,
But time hath rooted out my parentage,
And to the world and awkward casualties
Bound me in servitude. (*Aside*) I will desist.
But there is something glows upon my cheek,
And whispers in mine ear 'Go not till he speak.'

PERICLES

My fortunes, parentage, good parentage,
To equal mine? Was it not thus? What say you?

MARINA

I said, my lord, if you did know my parentage,
You would not do me violence.

PERICLES

I do think so. Pray you, turn your eyes upon me.
You're like something that—what countrywoman?
Here of these shores?

MARINA No, nor of any shores,
Yet I was mortally brought forth, and am
No other than I appear.

PERICLES

I am great with woe, and shall deliver weeping.
My dearest wife was like this maid, and such a one
My daughter might have been. My queen's square brows,
Her stature to an inch, as wand-like straight,
As silver-voiced, her eyes as jewel-like,
And cased as richly; in pace another Juno,

Who starves the ears she feeds, and makes them hungry
The more she gives them speech.—Where do you live?

MARINA
Where I am but a stranger. From the deck
You may discern the place.

PERICLES Where were you bred,
And how achieved you these endowments which
You make more rich to owe?

MARINA If I should tell
My history, it would seem like lies
Disdained in the reporting.

PERICLES Prithee speak.
Falseness cannot come from thee, for thou look'st
Modest as justice, and thou seem'st a palace
For the crownèd truth to dwell in. I will believe thee,
And make my senses credit thy relation
To points that seem impossible, for thou look'st
Like one I loved indeed. What were thy friends?
Didst thou not say, when I did push thee back—
Which was when I perceived thee—that thou cam'st
From good descending?

MARINA So indeed I did.

PERICLES
Report thy parentage. I think thou said'st
Thou hadst been tossed from wrong to injury,
And that thou thought'st thy griefs might equal mine,
If both were opened.

MARINA Some such thing I said,
And said no more but what my thoughts
Did warrant me was likely.

PERICLES Tell thy story.

If thine considered prove the thousandth part
Of my endurance, thou art a man, and I
Have suffered like a girl. Yet thou dost look
Like patience gazing on kings' graves, and smiling
Extremity out of act. What were thy friends?
How lost thou them? Thy name, my most kind virgin?
Recount, I do beseech thee. Come, sit by me.
She sits

MARINA
My name, sir, is Marina.

PERICLES O, I am mocked,
And thou by some incensèd god sent hither
To make the world to laugh at me.

MARINA Patience, good sir,
Or here I'll cease.

PERICLES Nay, I'll be patient.
Thou little know'st how thou dost startle me
To call thyself Marina.

MARINA The name
Was given me by one that had some power:
My father, and a king.

PERICLES How, a king's daughter,
And called Marina?

MARINA You said you would believe me,
But, not to be a troubler of your peace,
I will end here.

PERICLES But are you flesh and blood?
Have you a working pulse and are no fairy?
Motion as well? Speak on. Where were you born,
And wherefore called Marina?

MARINA Called Marina

For I was born at sea.

PERICLES At sea? What mother?

MARINA

My mother was the daughter of a king,
Who died the minute I was born, as my good nurse
Lychorida hath oft recounted weeping.

PERICLES

O, stop there a little! (*Aside*) This is the rarest dream
That e'er dulled sleep did mock sad fools withal.
This cannot be my daughter, buried. Well.
(*To Marina*) Where were you bred? I'll hear you more to th'
bottom
Of your story, and never interrupt you.

MARINA

You will scarce believe me. 'Twere best I did give o'er.

PERICLES

I will believe you by the syllable
Of what you shall deliver. Yet give me leave.
How came you in these parts? Where were you bred?

MARINA

The King my father did in Tarsus leave me,
Till cruel Cleon, with his wicked wife,
Did seek to murder me, and wooed a villain
To attempt the deed; who having drawn to do't,
A crew of pirates came and rescued me.
Brought me to Mytilene. But, good sir,
Whither will you have me? Why do you weep? It may be
You think me an impostor. No, good faith,
I am the daughter to King Pericles,
If good King Pericles be.

PERICLES (*rising*) Ho, Helicanus!

HELICANUS (*coming forward*) Calls my lord?

PERICLES

Thou art a grave and noble counsellor,
Most wise in gen'ral. Tell me if thou canst
What this maid is, or what is like to be,
That thus hath made me weep.

HELICANUS I know not.

But here's the regent, sir, of Mytilene
Speaks nobly of her.

LYSIMACHUS She would never tell

Her parentage. Being demanded that,
She would sit still and weep.

PERICLES

O Helicanus, strike me, honoured sir,
Give me a gash, put me to present pain,
Lest this great sea of joys rushing upon me
O'erbear the shores of my mortality
And drown me with their sweetness!
(*To Marina*) O, come hither,
Thou that begett'st him that did thee beget,
Thou that wast born at sea, buried at Tarsus,
And found at sea again!—O Helicanus,
Down on thy knees, thank the holy gods as loud
As thunder threatens us, this is Marina!
(*To Marina*)
What was thy mother's name? Tell me but that,
For truth can never be confirmed enough,
Though doubts did ever sleep.

MARINA First, sir, I pray,

What is your title?

PERICLES I am Pericles

Of Tyre. But tell me now my drowned queen's name.
As in the rest thou hast been godlike perfect,
So prove but true in that, thou art my daughter,
The heir of kingdoms, and another life
To Pericles thy father.

MARINA Is it no more
To be your daughter than to say my mother's name?
Thaisa was my mother, who did end
The minute I began.

PERICLES
Now blessing on thee! Rise. Thou art my child.
Give me fresh garments.—Mine own, Helicanus!
Not dead at Tarsus, as she should have been
By savage Cleon. She shall tell thee all,
When thou shalt kneel and justify in knowledge
She is thy very princess. Who is this?

HELICANUS
Sir, 'tis the governor of Mytilene,
Who, hearing of your melancholy state,
Did come to see you.

PERICLES (*to Lysimachus*) I embrace you, sir.—
Give me my robes. I am wild in my beholding.
O heavens, bless my girl!

Celestial music

But hark, what music?
Tell Helicanus, my Marina, tell him
O'er point by point, for yet he seems to doubt,
How sure you are my daughter. But what music?

HELICANUS My lord, I hear none.

PERICLES
None? The music of the spheres! List, my Marina.

LYSIMACHUS (*aside to the others*)
It is not good to cross him. Give him way.
PERICLES
Rar'st sounds. Do ye not hear?
LYSIMACHUS My lord, I hear.
PERICLES
Most heav'nly music.
It raps me unto list'ning, and thick slumber
Hangs upon mine eyelids. Let me rest.
He sleeps
LYSIMACHUS
A pillow for his head. Companion friends,
If this but answer to my just belief
I'll well remember you. So leave him all.

Sir Derek Jacobi, whose roles with the Royal Shakespeare Company include Benedick, Prospero, and Macbeth, played Pericles for the Prospect Players in 1973.

RICHARD JOHNSON

✡

Antony and Cleopatra

Act IV Scene 13

Mark Antony declares to his friend Scarus his belief that Cleopatra has betrayed him by withdrawing her troops during a battle.

ANTONY All is lost.
This foul Egyptian hath betrayèd me.
My fleet hath yielded to the foe, and yonder
They cast their caps up, and carouse together
Like friends long lost. Triple-turned whore! 'Tis thou
Hast sold me to this novice, and my heart
Makes only wars on thee. Bid them all fly;
For when I am revenged upon my charm,
I have done all. Bid them all fly. Be gone. *Exit Scarus*
O sun, thy uprise shall I see no more.
Fortune and Antony part here; even here
Do we shake hands. All come to this? The hearts
That spanieled me at heels, to whom I gave
Their wishes, do discandy, melt their sweets
On blossoming Caesar; and this pine is barked
That overtopped them all. Betrayed I am.
O this false soul of Egypt! This grave charm,
Whose eye becked forth my wars and called them home,

Whose bosom was my crownet, my chief end,
Like a right gipsy hath at fast and loose
Beguiled me to the very heart of loss.
What, Eros, Eros!
Enter Cleopatra
Ah, thou spell! Avaunt.

CLEOPATRA
Why is my lord enraged against his love?

ANTONY
Vanish, or I shall give thee thy deserving
And blemish Caesar's triumph. Let him take thee
And hoist thee up to the shouting plebeians;
Follow his chariot, like the greatest spot
Of all thy sex; most monster-like be shown
For poor'st diminutives, for dolts, and let
Patient Octavia plough thy visage up
With her preparèd nails. *Exit Cleopatra*
'Tis well thou'rt gone,
If it be well to live. But better 'twere
Thou fell'st into my fury, for one death
Might have prevented many. Eros, ho!
The shirt of Nessus is upon me. Teach me,
Alcides, thou mine ancestor, thy rage.
Let me lodge Lichas on the horns o'th' moon,
And with those hands that grasped the heaviest club
Subdue my worthiest self. The witch shall die.
To the young Roman boy she hath sold me, and I fall
Under this plot. She dies for't. Eros, ho!

Richard Johnson played Mark Antony for the Royal Shakespeare Company in both 1972 and 1992.

GEMMA JONES

✡

The Winter's Tale

Act V Scene 3

Leontes believes his wife, Hermione, died of grief after he repudiated their daughter, Perdita, as a bastard by his friend Polixenes. After sixteen years of penitence he is reconciled with Polixenes whose son Florizel is betrothed to Perdita. The faithful Paulina brings the royal party to see a statue of Hermione.

Enter Leontes, Polixenes, Florizel, Perdita, Camillo,
Paulina, Lords, and attendants

LEONTES
O grave and good Paulina, the great comfort
That I have had of thee!

PAULINA What, sovereign sir,
I did not well, I meant well. All my services
You have paid home, but that you have vouchsafed
With your crowned brother and these young contracted
Heirs of your kingdoms my poor house to visit,
It is a surplus of your grace which never
My life may last to answer.

LEONTES O Paulina,
We honour you with trouble. But we came
To see the statue of our queen. Your gallery

Have we passed through, not without much content
In many singularities; but we saw not
That which my daughter came to look upon,
The statue of her mother.

PAULINA As she lived peerless,
So her dead likeness I do well believe
Excels what ever yet you looked upon,
Or hand of man hath done. Therefore I keep it
Lonely, apart. But here it is. Prepare
To see the life as lively mocked as ever
Still sleep mocked death. Behold, and say 'tis well.
She draws a curtain and reveals the figure of Hermione, standing like a statue
I like your silence; it the more shows off
Your wonder. But yet speak; first you, my liege.
Comes it not something near?

LEONTES Her natural posture.
Chide me, dear stone, that I may say indeed
Thou art Hermione; or rather, thou art she
In thy not chiding, for she was as tender
As infancy and grace. But yet, Paulina,
Hermione was not so much wrinkled, nothing
So agèd as this seems.

POLIXENES O, not by much.

PAULINA
So much the more our carver's excellence,
Which lets go by some sixteen years, and makes her
As she lived now.

LEONTES As now she might have done,
So much to my good comfort as it is
Now piercing to my soul. O, thus she stood,

Even with such life of majesty—warm life,
As now it coldly stands—when first I wooed her.
I am ashamed. Does not the stone rebuke me
For being more stone than it? O royal piece!
There's magic in thy majesty, which has
My evils conjured to remembrance, and
From thy admiring daughter took the spirits,
Standing like stone with thee.

PERDITA And give me leave,
And do not say 'tis superstition, that
I kneel and then implore her blessing. Lady,
Dear Queen, that ended when I but began,
Give me that hand of yours to kiss.

PAULINA O, patience!
The statue is but newly fixed; the colour's
Not dry.

CAMILLO (*to Leontes*)
My lord, your sorrow was too sore laid on,
Which sixteen winters cannot blow away,
So many summers dry. Scarce any joy
Did ever so long live; no sorrow
But killed itself much sooner.

POLIXENES (*to Leontes*) Dear my brother,
Let him that was the cause of this have power
To take off so much grief from you as he
Will piece up in himself.

PAULINA (*to Leontes*) Indeed, my lord,
If I had thought the sight of my poor image
Would thus have wrought you—for the stone is mine—
I'd not have showed it.

She moves to draw the curtain

LEONTES Do not draw the curtain.
PAULINA No longer shall you gaze on't, lest your fancy
May think anon it moves.
LEONTES Let be, let be!
Would I were dead but that methinks already.
What was he that did make it? See, my lord,
Would you not deem it breathed, and that those veins
Did verily bear blood?
POLIXENES Masterly done.
The very life seems warm upon her lip.
LEONTES
The fixture of her eye has motion in't,
As we are mocked with art.
PAULINA I'll draw the curtain.
My lord's almost so far transported that
He'll think anon it lives.
LEONTES O sweet Paulina,
Make me to think so twenty years together.
No settled senses of the world can match
The pleasure of that madness. Let't alone.
PAULINA
I am sorry, sir, I have thus far stirred you; but
I could afflict you farther.
LEONTES Do, Paulina,
For this affliction has a taste as sweet
As any cordial comfort. Still methinks
There is an air comes from her. What fine chisel
Could ever yet cut breath? Let no man mock me,
For I will kiss her.
PAULINA Good my lord, forbear.
The ruddiness upon her lip is wet.

You'll mar it if you kiss it, stain your own
With oily painting. Shall I draw the curtain?

LEONTES No, not these twenty years.

PERDITA So long could I
Stand by, a looker-on.

PAULINA Either forbear,
Quit presently the chapel, or resolve you
For more amazement. If you can behold it,
I'll make the statue move indeed, descend,
And take you by the hand. But then you'll think—
Which I protest against—I am assisted
By wicked powers.

LEONTES What you can make her do
I am content to look on; what to speak,
I am content to hear; for 'tis as easy
To make her speak as move.

PAULINA It is required
You do awake your faith. Then, all stand still.
Or those that think it is unlawful business
I am about, let them depart.

LEONTES Proceed.
No foot shall stir.

PAULINA Music; awake her; strike!

Music sounds

(*To Hermione*) 'Tis time. Descend. Be stone no more.
Approach.
Strike all that look upon with marvel. Come,
I'll fill your grave up. Stir. Nay, come away.
Bequeath to death your numbness, for from him
Dear life redeems you. (*To Leontes*) You perceive she stirs.

Hermione slowly descends

Start not. Her actions shall be holy as
You hear my spell is lawful. Do not shun her
Until you see her die again, for then
You kill her double. Nay, present your hand.
When she was young, you wooed her. Now, in age,
Is she become the suitor?

LEONTES O, she's warm!
If this be magic, let it be an art
Lawful as eating.

POLIXENES She embraces him.

CAMILLO She hangs about his neck.
If she pertain to life, let her speak too.

POLIXENES
Ay, and make it manifest where she has lived,
Or how stol'n from the dead.

PAULINA That she is living,
Were it but told you, should be hooted at
Like an old tale. But it appears she lives,
Though yet she speak not. Mark a little while.
(*To Perdita*) Please you to interpose, fair madam. Kneel,
And pray your mother's blessing.—Turn, good lady,
Our Perdita is found.

HERMIONE You gods, look down,
And from your sacred vials pour your graces
Upon my daughter's head.—Tell me, mine own,
Where hast thou been preserved? Where lived? How found
Thy father's court? For thou shalt hear that I,
Knowing by Paulina that the oracle
Gave hope thou wast in being, have preserved
Myself to see the issue.

PAULINA There's time enough for that,
Lest they desire upon this push to trouble
Your joys with like relation. Go together,
You precious winners all; your exultation
Partake to everyone. I, an old turtle,
Will wing me to some withered bough, and there
My mate, that's never to be found again,
Lament till I am lost.

LEONTES O peace, Paulina!
Thou shouldst a husband take by my consent,
As I by thine a wife. This is a match,
And made between 's by vows. Thou hast found mine,
But how is to be questioned, for I saw her,
As I thought, dead, and have in vain said many
A prayer upon her grave. I'll not seek far—
For him, I partly know his mind—to find thee
An honourable husband. Come, Camillo,
And take her by the hand, whose worth and honesty
Is richly noted, and here justified
By us, a pair of kings. Let's from this place.
(*To Hermione*) What, look upon my brother. Both your
pardons,
That e'er I put between your holy looks
My ill suspicion. This' your son-in-law
And son unto the King, whom heavens directing
Is troth-plight to your daughter. Good Paulina,
Lead us from hence, where we may leisurely
Each one demand and answer to his part
Performed in this wide gap of time since first
We were dissevered. Hastily lead away. *Exeunt*

A Midsummer Night's Dream

Act II Scene 1

Oberon and Titania, King and Queen of the Fairies, meet by moonlight

OBERON
Ill met by moonlight, proud Titania.
TITANIA
What, jealous Oberon?—Fairies, skip hence.
I have forsworn his bed and company.
OBERON
Tarry, rash wanton. Am not I thy lord?
TITANIA
Then I must be thy lady; but I know
When thou hast stol'n away from fairyland
And in the shape of Corin sat all day,
Playing on pipes of corn, and versing love
To amorous Phillida. Why art thou here
Come from the farthest step of India,
But that, forsooth, the bouncing Amazon,
Your buskined mistress and your warrior love,
To Theseus must be wedded, and you come
To give their bed joy and prosperity?
OBERON
How canst thou thus for shame, Titania,
Glance at my credit with Hippolyta,
Knowing I know thy love to Theseus?
Didst not thou lead him through the glimmering night
From Perigouna whom he ravishèd,

And make him with fair Aegles break his faith,
With Ariadne and Antiopa?

TITANIA

These are the forgeries of jealousy,
And never since the middle summer's spring
Met we on hill, in dale, forest, or mead,
By pavèd fountain or by rushy brook,
Or in the beachèd margin of the sea
To dance our ringlets to the whistling wind,
But with thy brawls thou hast disturbed our sport.
Therefore the winds, piping to us in vain,
As in revenge have sucked up from the sea
Contagious fogs which, falling in the land,
Hath every pelting river made so proud
That they have overborne their continents.
The ox hath therefore stretched his yoke in vain,
The ploughman lost his sweat, and the green corn
Hath rotted ere his youth attained a beard.
The fold stands empty in the drownèd field,
And crows are fatted with the murrain flock.
The nine men's morris is filled up with mud,
And the quaint mazes in the wanton green
For lack of tread are undistinguishable.
The human mortals want their winter cheer.
No night is now with hymn or carol blessed.
Therefore the moon, the governess of floods,
Pale in her anger washes all the air,
That rheumatic diseases do abound;
And thorough this distemperature we see
The seasons alter: hoary-headed frosts
Fall in the fresh lap of the crimson rose,

And on old Hiems' thin and icy crown
An odorous chaplet of sweet summer buds
Is, as in mock'ry, set. The spring, the summer,
The childing autumn, angry winter change
Their wonted liveries, and the mazèd world
By their increase now knows not which is which;
And this same progeny of evils comes
From our debate, from our dissension.
We are their parents and original.

OBERON

Do you amend it, then. It lies in you.
Why should Titania cross her Oberon?
I do but beg a little changeling boy
To be my henchman.

TITANIA Set your heart at rest.

The fairyland buys not the child of me.
His mother was a vot'ress of my order,
And in the spicèd Indian air by night
Full often hath she gossiped by my side,
And sat with me on Neptune's yellow sands,
Marking th' embarkèd traders on the flood,
When we have laughed to see the sails conceive
And grow big-bellied with the wanton wind,
Which she with pretty and with swimming gait
Following, her womb then rich with my young squire,
Would imitate, and sail upon the land
To fetch me trifles, and return again
As from a voyage, rich with merchandise.
But she, being mortal, of that boy did die;
And for her sake do I rear up her boy;
And for her sake I will not part with him.

OBERON

How long within this wood intend you stay?

TITANIA

Perchance till after Theseus' wedding day.
If you will patiently dance in our round,
And see our moonlight revels, go with us.
If not, shun me, and I will spare your haunts.

Gemma Jones played Hermione with the Royal Shakespeare Company in 1981, and Titania in 1973.

GRIFFITH JONES

✡

Hamlet

Act I Scene 5

The Ghost of Hamlet's father tells Hamlet of his murder

But soft, methinks I scent the morning's air.
Brief let me be. Sleeping within mine orchard,
My custom always in the afternoon,
Upon my secure hour thy uncle stole
With juice of cursèd hebenon in a vial,
And in the porches of mine ears did pour
The leperous distilment, whose effect
Holds such an enmity with blood of man
That swift as quicksilver it courses through
The natural gates and alleys of the body,
And with a sudden vigour it doth posset
And curd, like eager droppings into milk,
The thin and wholesome blood. So did it mine;
And a most instant tetter barked about,
Most lazar-like, with vile and loathsome crust,
All my smooth body.
Thus was I, sleeping, by a brother's hand
Of life, of crown, of queen at once dispatched,
Cut off even in the blossoms of my sin,

Unhouseled, dis-appointed, unaneled,
No reck'ning made, but sent to my account
With all my imperfections on my head.

Henry IV, Part Two

Act V, Scene 2

The Lord Chief Justice, meeting the newly crowned King Henry V, defends himself against Henry's charge that he did 'rate, rebuke, and roughly send to prison Th'immediate heir of England.'

LORD CHIEF JUSTICE

I then did use the person of your father.
The image of his power lay then in me;
And in th'administration of his law,
Whiles I was busy for the commonwealth,
Your highness pleasèd to forget my place,
The majesty and power of law and justice,
The image of the King whom I presented,
And struck me in my very seat of judgement;
Whereon, as an offender to your father,
I gave bold way to my authority
And did commit you. If the deed were ill,
Be you contented, wearing now the garland,
To have a son set your decrees at naught—
To pluck down justice from your awe-full bench,
To trip the course of law, and blunt the sword
That guards the peace and safety of your person,

Nay, more, to spurn at your most royal image,
And mock your workings in a second body?
Question your royal thoughts, make the case yours,
Be now the father, and propose a son;
Hear your own dignity so much profaned,
See your most dreadful laws so loosely slighted,
Behold yourself so by a son disdained;
And then imagine me taking your part,
And in your power soft silencing your son.
After this cold considerance, sentence me;
And, as you are a king, speak in your state
What I have done that misbecame my place,
My person, or my liege's sovereignty.

Griffith Jones played the Ghost and the Lord Chief Justice with the Royal Shakespeare Company in 1975.

CHARLES KAY

✡

Richard III

Act I Scene 4

The Duke of Clarence is imprisoned in the Tower of London on the orders of his brother Richard, Duke of Gloucester, who has hired men to murder him.

Enter George Duke of Clarence and Sir Robert Brackenbury

BRACKENBURY

Why looks your grace so heavily today?

CLARENCE

O I have passed a miserable night,
So full of fearful dreams, of ugly sights,
That as I am a Christian faithful man,
I would not spend another such a night
Though 'twere to buy a world of happy days,
So full of dismal terror was the time.

BRACKENBURY

What was your dream, my lord? I pray you, tell me.

CLARENCE

Methoughts that I had broken from the Tower,
And was embarked to cross to Burgundy,
And in my company my brother Gloucester,
Who from my cabin tempted me to walk

Upon the hatches; there we looked toward England,
And cited up a thousand heavy times
During the wars of York and Lancaster
That had befall'n us. As we paced along
Upon the giddy footing of the hatches,
Methought that Gloucester stumbled, and in falling
Struck me—that sought to stay him—overboard
Into the tumbling billows of the main.
O Lord! Methought what pain it was to drown,
What dreadful noise of waters in my ears,
What sights of ugly death within my eyes.
Methoughts I saw a thousand fearful wrecks,
Ten thousand men that fishes gnawed upon,
Wedges of gold, great ouches, heaps of pearl,
Inestimable stones, unvalued jewels,
All scattered in the bottom of the sea.
Some lay in dead men's skulls; and in those holes
Where eyes did once inhabit, there were crept—
As 'twere in scorn of eyes—reflecting gems,
Which wooed the slimy bottom of the deep
And mocked the dead bones that lay scattered by.

BRACKENBURY

Had you such leisure in the time of death,
To gaze upon these secrets of the deep?

CLARENCE

Methought I had, and often did I strive
To yield the ghost, but still the envious flood
Stopped-in my soul and would not let it forth
To find the empty, vast, and wand'ring air,
But smothered it within my panting bulk,
Who almost burst to belch it in the sea.

BRACKENBURY

Awaked you not in this sore agony?

CLARENCE

No, no, my dream was lengthened after life.
O then began the tempest to my soul!
I passed, methought, the melancholy flood,
With that sour ferryman which poets write of,
Unto the kingdom of perpetual night.
The first that there did greet my stranger soul
Was my great father-in-law, renownèd Warwick,
Who cried aloud, 'What scourge for perjury
Can this dark monarchy afford false Clarence?'
And so he vanished. Then came wand'ring by
A shadow like an angel, with bright hair,
Dabbled in blood, and he shrieked out aloud,
'Clarence is come: false, fleeting, perjured Clarence,
That stabbed me in the field by Tewkesbury.
Seize on him, furies! Take him unto torment!'
With that, methoughts a legion of foul fiends
Environed me, and howlèd in mine ears
Such hideous cries that with the very noise
I trembling waked, and for a season after
Could not believe but that I was in hell,
Such terrible impression made my dream.

BRACKENBURY

No marvel, lord, though it affrighted you;
I am afraid, methinks, to hear you tell it.

CLARENCE

Ah, Brackenbury, I have done these things,
That now give evidence against my soul,
For Edward's sake; and see how he requites me.

Keeper, I pray thee, sit by me awhile.
My soul is heavy, and I fain would sleep.

Charles Kay played Clarence with the Royal Shakespeare Company in 1963.

BEN KINGSLEY

✡

Othello

Act I Scene 3

Othello tells the Senate of Venice how he wooed and won Desdemona, daughter of Brabantio.

OTHELLO

Her father loved me, oft invited me,
Still questioned me the story of my life
From year to year, the battles, sieges, fortunes
That I have passed.
I ran it through even from my boyish days
To th' very moment that he bade me tell it,
Wherein I spoke of most disastrous chances,
Of moving accidents by flood and field,
Of hair-breadth scapes i'th' imminent deadly breach,
Of being taken by the insolent foe
And sold to slavery, of my redemption thence,
And portance in my traveller's history,
Wherein of antres vast and deserts idle,
Rough quarries, rocks, and hills whose heads touch heaven,
It was my hint to speak. Such was my process,
And of the cannibals that each other eat,
The Anthropophagi, and men whose heads

Do grow beneath their shoulders. These things to hear
Would Desdemona seriously incline,
But still the house affairs would draw her thence,
Which ever as she could with haste dispatch
She'd come again, and with a greedy ear
Devour up my discourse; which I observing,
Took once a pliant hour, and found good means
To draw from her a prayer of earnest heart
That I would all my pilgrimage dilate,
Whereof by parcels she had something heard,
But not intentively. I did consent,
And often did beguile her of her tears
When I did speak of some distressful stroke
That my youth suffered. My story being done,
She gave me for my pains a world of kisses.
She swore in faith 'twas strange, 'twas passing strange,
'Twas pitiful, 'twas wondrous pitiful.
She wished she had not heard it, yet she wished
That heaven had made her such a man. She thankèd me,
And bade me, if I had a friend that loved her,
I should but teach him how to tell my story,
And that would woo her. Upon this hint I spake.
She loved me for the dangers I had passed,
And I loved her that she did pity them.
This only is the witchcraft I have used.

Ben Kingsley played Othello for the Royal Shakespeare Company in 1985.

JANE LAPOTAIRE

✡

Twelfth Night

Act I Scene 5

Viola, disguised as the page Cesario, comes to woo Olivia (who wears a veil) on behalf of Orsino.

VIOLA The honourable lady of the house, which is she?

OLIVIA Speak to me, I shall answer for her. Your will.

VIOLA Most radiant, exquisite, and unmatchable beauty.—I pray you, tell me if this be the lady of the house, for I never saw her. I would be loath to cast away my speech, for besides that it is excellently well penned, I have taken great pains to con it. Good beauties, let me sustain no scorn; I am very 'countable, even to the least sinister usage.

OLIVIA Whence came you, sir?

VIOLA I can say little more than I have studied, and that question's out of my part. Good gentle one, give me modest assurance if you be the lady of the house, that I may proceed in my speech.

OLIVIA Are you a comedian?

VIOLA No, my profound heart; and yet—by the very fangs of malice I swear—I am not that I play. Are you the lady of the house?

OLIVIA If I do not usurp myself, I am.

VIOLA Most certain if you are she you do usurp yourself, for what is yours to bestow is not yours to reserve. But this is from my commission. I will on with my speech in your praise, and then show you the heart of my message.

OLIVIA Come to what is important in't, I forgive you the praise.

VIOLA Alas, I took great pains to study it, and 'tis poetical.

OLIVIA It is the more like to be feigned, I pray you keep it in. I heard you were saucy at my gates, and allowed your approach rather to wonder at you than to hear you. If you be not mad, be gone. If you have reason, be brief. 'Tis not that time of moon with me to make one in so skipping a dialogue.

MARIA Will you hoist sail, sir? Here lies your way.

VIOLA No, good swabber, I am to hull here a little longer. (*To Olivia*) Some mollification for your giant, sweet lady. Tell me your mind, I am a messenger.

OLIVIA Sure, you have some hideous matter to deliver when the courtesy of it is so fearful. Speak your office.

VIOLA It alone concerns your ear. I bring no overture of war, no taxation of homage. I hold the olive in my hand. My words are as full of peace as matter.

OLIVIA Yet you began rudely. What are you? What would you?

VIOLA The rudeness that hath appeared in me have I learned from my entertainment. What I am and what I would are as secret as maidenhead; to your ears, divinity; to any others', profanation.

OLIVIA (*to Maria and attendants*) Give us the place alone, we will hear this divinity.

Exeunt Maria and attendants

Now sir, what is your text?

VIOLA Most sweet lady—

OLIVIA A comfortable doctrine, and much may be said of it. Where lies your text?

VIOLA In Orsino's bosom.

OLIVIA In his bosom? In what chapter of his bosom?

VIOLA To answer by the method, in the first of his heart.

OLIVIA O, I have read it. It is heresy. Have you no more to say?

VIOLA Good madam, let me see your face.

OLIVIA Have you any commission from your lord to negotiate with my face? You are now out of your text. But we will draw the curtain and show you the picture.

She unveils

Look you, sir, such a one I was this present. Is't not well done?

VIOLA Excellently done, if God did all.

OLIVIA 'Tis in grain, sir, 'twill endure wind and weather.

VIOLA

'Tis beauty truly blent, whose red and white
Nature's own sweet and cunning hand laid on.
Lady, you are the cruell'st she alive
If you will lead these graces to the grave
And leave the world no copy.

OLIVIA O sir, I will not be so hard-hearted. I will give out divers schedules of my beauty. It shall be inventoried and every particle and utensil labelled to my will, as, item, two lips, indifferent red; item, two grey eyes, with lids to them; item, one neck, one chin, and so forth. Were you sent hither to praise me?

VIOLA

I see you what you are, you are too proud,
But if you were the devil, you are fair.

My lord and master loves you. O, such love
Could be but recompensed though you were crowned
The nonpareil of beauty.

OLIVIA How does he love me?

VIOLA

With adorations, fertile tears,
With groans that thunder love, with sighs of fire.

OLIVIA

Your lord does know my mind, I cannot love him.
Yet I suppose him virtuous, know him noble,
Of great estate, of fresh and stainless youth,
In voices well divulged, free, learned, and valiant,
And in dimension and the shape of nature
A gracious person; but yet I cannot love him.
He might have took his answer long ago.

VIOLA

If I did love you in my master's flame,
With such a suff'ring, such a deadly life,
In your denial I would find no sense,
I would not understand it.

OLIVIA Why, what would you?

VIOLA

Make me a willow cabin at your gate
And call upon my soul within the house,
Write loyal cantons of contemnèd love,
And sing them loud even in the dead of night;
Halloo your name to the reverberate hills,
And make the babbling gossip of the air
Cry out 'Olivia!' O, you should not rest
Between the elements of air and earth
But you should pity me.

Henry VIII (All is True)

Act II Scene 4

Katherine of Aragon, Henry VIII's wife, defends the legality of her twenty-year-old marriage which has been questioned by Cardinal Wolsey

SCRIBE (*to the Crier*)
Say, 'Henry, King of England, come into the court'.
CRIER
Henry, King of England, come into the court.
KING HENRY Here.
SCRIBE (*to the Crier*)
Say, 'Katherine, Queen of England, come into the court'.
CRIER
Katherine, Queen of England, come into the court.
The Queen makes no answer, but rises out of her chair, goes about the court, comes to the King, and kneels at his feet. Then she speaks
QUEEN KATHERINE
Sir, I desire you do me right and justice,
And to bestow your pity on me; for
I am a most poor woman, and a stranger,
Born out of your dominions, having here
No judge indifferent, nor no more assurance
Of equal friendship and proceeding. Alas, sir,
In what have I offended you? What cause
Hath my behaviour given to your displeasure
That thus you should proceed to put me off,
And take your good grace from me? Heaven witness

I have been to you a true and humble wife,
At all times to your will conformable,
Ever in fear to kindle your dislike,
Yea, subject to your countenance, glad or sorry
As I saw it inclined. When was the hour
I ever contradicted your desire,
Or made it not mine too? Or which of your friends
Have I not strove to love, although I knew
He were mine enemy? What friend of mine
That had to him derived your anger did I
Continue in my liking? Nay, gave notice
He was from thence discharged? Sir, call to mind
That I have been your wife in this obedience
Upward of twenty years, and have been blessed
With many children by you. If, in the course
And process of this time, you can report—
And prove it, too—against mine honour aught,
My bond to wedlock, or my love and duty
Against your sacred person, in God's name
Turn me away, and let the foul'st contempt
Shut door upon me, and so give me up
To the sharp'st kind of justice. Please you, sir,
The King your father was reputed for
A prince most prudent, of an excellent
And unmatched wit and judgement. Ferdinand
My father, King of Spain, was reckoned one
The wisest prince that there had reigned by many
A year before. It is not to be questioned
That they had gathered a wise council to them
Of every realm, that did debate this business,
Who deemed our marriage lawful. Wherefore I humbly

Beseech you, sir, to spare me till I may
Be by my friends in Spain advised, whose counsel
I will implore. If not, i'th' name of God,
Your pleasure be fulfilled.

CARDINAL WOLSEY You have here, lady,
And of your choice, these reverend fathers, men
Of singular integrity and learning,
Yea, the elect o'th' land, who are assembled
To plead your cause. It shall be therefore bootless
That longer you desire the court, as well
For your own quiet, as to rectify
What is unsettled in the King.

CARDINAL CAMPEIUS His grace
Hath spoken well and justly. Therefore, madam,
It's fit this royal session do proceed,
And that without delay their arguments
Be now produced and heard.

QUEEN KATHERINE (*to Wolsey*) Lord Cardinal,
To you I speak.

CARDINAL WOLSEY
Your pleasure, madam.

QUEEN KATHERINE Sir,
I am about to weep, but thinking that
We are a queen, or long have dreamed so, certain
The daughter of a king, my drops of tears
I'll turn to sparks of fire.

CARDINAL WOLSEY Be patient yet.

QUEEN KATHERINE
I will when you are humble! Nay, before,
Or God will punish me. I do believe,
Induced by potent circumstances, that

You are mine enemy, and make my challenge
You shall not be my judge. For it is you
Have blown this coal betwixt my lord and me,
Which God's dew quench. Therefore I say again,
I utterly abhor, yea, from my soul,
Refuse you for my judge, whom yet once more
I hold my most malicious foe, and think not
At all a friend to truth.

CARDINAL WOLSEY I do profess
You speak not like yourself, who ever yet
Have stood to charity, and displayed th'effects
Of disposition gentle and of wisdom
O'er-topping woman's power. Madam, you do me wrong.
I have no spleen against you, nor injustice
For you or any. How far I have proceeded,
Or how far further shall, is warranted
By a commission from the consistory,
Yea, the whole consistory of Rome. You charge me
That I 'have blown this coal'. I do deny it.
The King is present. If it be known to him
That I gainsay my deed, how may he wound,
And worthily, my falsehood—yea, as much
As you have done my truth. If he know
That I am free of your report, he knows
I am not of your wrong. Therefore in him
It lies to cure me, and the cure is to
Remove these thoughts from you. The which before
His highness shall speak in, I do beseech
You, gracious madam, to unthink your speaking,
And to say so no more.

QUEEN KATHERINE My lord, my lord—

I am a simple woman, much too weak
T'oppose your cunning. You're meek and humble-
mouthed;
You sign your place and calling, in full seeming,
With meekness and humility—but your heart
Is crammed with arrogancy, spleen, and pride.
You have by fortune and his highness' favours
Gone slightly o'er low steps, and now are mounted
Where powers are your retainers, and your words,
Domestics to you, serve your will as't please
Yourself pronounce their office. I must tell you,
You tender more your person's honour than
Your high profession spiritual, that again
I do refuse you for my judge, and here,
Before you all, appeal unto the Pope,
To bring my whole cause 'fore his holiness,
And to be judged by him.

She curtsies to the King and begins to depart

CARDINAL CAMPEIUS The Queen is obstinate,
Stubborn to justice, apt to accuse it, and
Disdainful to be tried by't. 'Tis not well.
She's going away.

KING HENRY (*to the Crier*) Call her again.

CRIER
Katherine, Queen of England, come into the court.

GRIFFITH (*to the Queen*) Madam, you are called back.

QUEEN KATHERINE
What need you note it? Pray you keep your way.
When you are called, return. Now the Lord help.
They vex me past my patience. Pray you, pass on.
I will not tarry; no, nor ever more

Upon this business my appearance make
In any of their courts.
Exeunt Queen Katherine and her attendants

Jane Lapotaire played Viola with the Royal Shakespeare Company in 1974, and Queen Katherine in 1997.

BARBARA LEIGH-HUNT

✡

The Merry Wives of Windsor

Act II Scene 1

Mistress Page and Mistress Ford discover that Sir John Falstaff has sent identical love letters to both of them.

Enter Mistress Page, with a letter

MISTRESS PAGE What, have I scaped love-letters in the holiday time of my beauty, and am I now a subject for them? Let me see.

She reads

'Ask me no reason why I love you, for though Love use Reason for his precision, he admits him not for his counsellor. You are not young; no more am I. Go to, then, there's sympathy. You are merry; so am I. Ha, ha, then, there's more sympathy. You love sack, and so do I. Would you desire better sympathy? Let it suffice thee, Mistress Page, at the least if the love of soldier can suffice, that I love thee. I will not say "pity me"—'tis not a soldier-like phrase—but I say "love me".

By me, thine own true knight,
By day or night
Or any kind of light,
With all his might
For thee to fight,
John Falstaff.'

What a Herod of Jewry is this! O, wicked, wicked world! One that is well-nigh worn to pieces with age, to show himself a young gallant! What an unweighed behaviour hath this Flemish drunkard picked, i'th' devil's name, out of my conversation, that he dares in this manner assay me? Why, he hath not been thrice in my company. What should I say to him? I was then frugal of my mirth, heaven forgive me. Why, I'll exhibit a bill in the Parliament for the putting down of men. O God, that I knew how to be revenged on him! For revenged I will be, as sure as his guts are made of puddings.

Enter Mistress Ford

MISTRESS FORD Mistress Page! By my faith, I was going to your house.

MISTRESS PAGE And by my faith, I was coming to you. You look very ill.

MISTRESS FORD Nay, I'll ne'er believe that: I have to show to the contrary.

MISTRESS PAGE Faith, but you do, in my mind.

MISTRESS FORD Well, I do, then. Yet I say I could show you to the contrary. O Mistress Page, give me some counsel.

MISTRESS PAGE What's the matter, woman?

MISTRESS FORD O woman, if it were not for one trifling respect, I could come to such honour!

MISTRESS PAGE Hang the trifle, woman; take the honour. What is it? Dispense with trifles. What is it?

MISTRESS FORD If I would but go to hell for an eternal moment or so, I could be knighted.

MISTRESS PAGE What? Thou liest! Sir Alice Ford? These knights will hack, and so thou shouldst not alter the article of thy gentry.

MISTRESS FORD We burn daylight. Here: read, read.

She gives Mistress Page a letter

Perceive how I might be knighted.

Mistress Page reads

I shall think the worse of fat men as long as I have an eye to make difference of men's liking. And yet he would not swear, praised women's modesty, and gave such orderly and well-behaved reproof to all uncomeliness that I would have sworn his disposition would have gone to the truth of his words. But they do no more adhere and keep place together than the hundred and fifty psalms to the tune of 'Green-sleeves'. What tempest, I trow, threw this whale, with so many tuns of oil in his belly, ashore at Windsor? How shall I be revenged on him? I think the best way were to entertain him with hope, till the wicked fire of lust have melted him in his own grease. Did you ever hear the like?

MISTRESS PAGE Letter for letter, but that the name of Page and Ford differs.

She gives Mistress Ford her letter

To thy great comfort in this mystery of ill opinions, here's the twin brother of thy letter. But let thine inherit first, for I protest mine never shall. I warrant he hath a thousand of these letters, writ with blank space for different names—sure, more, and these are of the second edition. He will print them, out of doubt—for he cares not what he puts into the press when he would put us two. I had rather be a giantess, and lie under Mount Pelion. Well, I will find you twenty lascivious turtles ere one chaste man.

MISTRESS FORD Why, this is the very same: the very hand, the very words. What doth he think of us?

MISTRESS PAGE Nay, I know not. It makes me almost ready to wrangle with mine own honesty. I'll entertain myself like one that I am not acquainted withal; for, sure, unless he know some strain in me that I know not myself, he would never have boarded me in this fury.

MISTRESS FORD 'Boarding' call you it? I'll be sure to keep him above deck.

MISTRESS PAGE So will I. If he come under my hatches, I'll never to sea again. Let's be revenged on him. Let's appoint him a meeting, give him a show of comfort in his suit, and lead him on with a fine baited delay till he hath pawned his horses to mine Host of the Garter.

MISTRESS FORD Nay, I will consent to act any villainy against him that may not sully the chariness of our honesty. O that my husband saw this letter! It would give eternal food to his jealousy.

The Two Gentlemen of Verona

Act I Scene 2

Proteus on young love

O, how this spring of love resembleth
The uncertain glory of an April day,
Which now shows all the beauty of the sun,
And by and by a cloud takes all away.

Barbara Leigh-Hunt played Mistress Ford with the Royal Shakespeare Company in 1975

FINBAR LYNCH

✡

The Two Gentlemen of Verona

Act II Scene 4

Proteus, until now in love with Julia, expresses his feelings on realizing that he has fallen for Silvia, beloved by his dearest friend Valentine.

Even as one heat another heat expels,
Or as one nail by strength drives out another,
So the remembrance of my former love
Is by a newer object quite forgotten.
Is it mine eye, or Valentine's praise,
Her true perfection, or my false transgression
That makes me, reasonless, to reason thus?
She is fair, and so is Julia that I love—
That I did love, for now my love is thawed,
Which like a waxen image 'gainst a fire
Bears no impression of the thing it was.
Methinks my zeal to Valentine is cold,
And that I love him not as I was wont.
O, but I love his lady too-too much,
And that's the reason I love him so little.
How shall I dote on her with more advice,
That thus without advice begin to love her?
'Tis but her picture I have yet beheld,

And that hath dazzled my reason's light.
But when I look on her perfections
There is no reason but I shall be blind.
If I can check my erring love I will,
If not, to compass her I'll use my skill.

A Midsummer Night's Dream

Act V Scene 2

Robin Goodfellow, the puck, prepares the way for the entrance of the King and Queen of the fairies at the end of the play.

Now the hungry lion roars,
　And the wolf behowls the moon,
Whilst the heavy ploughman snores,
　All with weary task fordone.
Now the wasted brands do glow
　Whilst the screech-owl, screeching loud,
Puts the wretch that lies in woe
　In remembrance of a shroud.
Now it is the time of night
　That the graves, all gaping wide,
Every one lets forth his sprite
　In the churchway paths to glide;
And we fairies that do run
　By the triple Hecate's team
From the presence of the sun,
　Following darkness like a dream,

Now are frolic. Not a mouse
Shall disturb this hallowed house.
I am sent with broom before
To sweep the dust behind the door.

Finbar (Barry) Lynch played Proteus with the Royal Shakespeare Company in 1991, and Robin Goodfellow (or Puck) in 1994.

ALEC McCOWEN

☆

Troilus and Cressida

Act IV Scene 5

Cressida is obliged to leave Troy and her lover Troilus.

CRESSIDA
And is it true that I must go from Troy?
TROILUS
A hateful truth.
CRESSIDA What, and from Troilus too?
TROILUS
From Troy and Troilus.
CRESSIDA Is't possible?
TROILUS
And suddenly—where injury of chance
Puts back leave-taking, jostles roughly by
All time of pause, rudely beguiles our lips
Of all rejoindure, forcibly prevents
Our locked embrasures, strangles our dear vows
Even in the birth of our own labouring breath.
We two, that with so many thousand sighs
Did buy each other, must poorly sell ourselves
With the rude brevity and discharge of one.
Injurious Time now with a robber's haste

Crams his rich thiev'ry up, he knows not how.
As many farewells as be stars in heaven,
With distinct breath and consigned kisses to them,
He fumbles up into a loose adieu
And scants us with a single famished kiss,
Distasted with the salt of broken tears.

Henry IV, Part One

Act I Scene 3

Harry Percy, known as Hotspur, meditates on honour.

By heaven, methinks it were an easy leap
To pluck bright honour from the pale-faced moon,
Or dive into the bottom of the deep,
Where fathom-line could never touch the ground,
And pluck up drownèd honour by the locks,
So he that doth redeem her thence might wear,
Without corrival, all her dignities.
But out upon this half-faced fellowship!

Alec McCowen's roles with the Royal Shakespeare Company include Antipholus of Syracuse, the Fool in *King Lear*, and Prospero.

IAN McKELLEN

☆

Macbeth

Act II, Scene 2

Macbeth has just murdered King Duncan.

MACBETH

I have done the deed. Didst thou not hear a noise?

LADY MACBETH

I heard the owl scream and the crickets cry.
Did not you speak?

MACBETH When?

LADY MACBETH Now.

MACBETH As I descended?

LADY MACBETH Ay.

MACBETH Hark!—Who lies i'th' second chamber?

LADY MACBETH Donalbain.

MACBETH (*looking at his hands*) This is a sorry sight.

LADY MACBETH

A foolish thought, to say a sorry sight.

MACBETH

There's one did laugh in's sleep, and one cried 'Murder!'
That they did wake each other. I stood and heard them.
But they did say their prayers and addressed them
Again to sleep.

LADY MACBETH There are two lodged together.

MACBETH

One cried 'God bless us' and 'Amen' the other,
As they had seen me with these hangman's hands.
List'ning their fear I could not say 'Amen'
When they did say 'God bless us.'

LADY MACBETH Consider it not so deeply.

MACBETH

But wherefore could not I pronounce 'Amen'?
I had most need of blessing, and 'Amen'
Stuck in my throat.

LADY MACBETH These deeds must not be thought
After these ways. So, it will make us mad.

MACBETH

Methought I heard a voice cry 'Sleep no more,
Macbeth does murder sleep'—the innocent sleep,
Sleep that knits up the ravelled sleave of care,
The death of each day's life, sore labour's bath,
Balm of hurt minds, great nature's second course,
Chief nourisher in life's feast—

LADY MACBETH What do you mean?

MACBETH

Still it cried 'Sleep no more' to all the house,
'Glamis hath murdered sleep, and therefore Cawdor
Shall sleep no more, Macbeth shall sleep no more.'

LADY MACBETH

Who was it that thus cried? Why, worthy thane,
You do unbend your noble strength to think
So brain-sickly of things. Go get some water
And wash this filthy witness from your hand.
Why did you bring these daggers from the place?

They must lie there. Go, carry them, and smear
The sleepy grooms with blood.

MACBETH I'll go no more.
I am afraid to think what I have done,
Look on't again I dare not.

LADY MACBETH Infirm of purpose!
Give me the daggers. The sleeping and the dead
Are but as pictures. 'Tis the eye of childhood
That fears a painted devil. If he do bleed
I'll gild the faces of the grooms withal,
For it must seem their guilt. *Exit*

Knock within

MACBETH Whence is that knocking?—
How is't with me when every noise appals me?
What hands are here! Ha, they pluck out mine eyes.
Will all great Neptune's ocean wash this blood
Clean from my hand? No, this my hand will rather
The multitudinous seas incarnadine,
Making the green one red.

The Winter's Tale

Act I Scene 2

Leontes, watching the friendly behaviour of his wife, Hermione, with his friend Polixenes, suspects her of infidelity.

LEONTES (*aside*) Too hot, too hot:
To mingle friendship farre is mingling bloods.

I have tremor cordis on me. My heart dances,
But not for joy, not joy. This entertainment
May a free face put on, derive a liberty
From heartiness, from bounty, fertile bosom,
And well become the agent. 'T may, I grant.
But to be paddling palms and pinching fingers,
As now they are, and making practised smiles
As in a looking-glass; and then to sigh, as 'twere
The mort o'th' deer—O, that is entertainment
My bosom likes not, nor my brows.—Mamillius,
Art thou my boy?

MAMILLIUS Ay, my good lord.

LEONTES I' fecks,
Why, that's my bawcock. What? Hast smutched thy nose?
They say it is a copy out of mine. Come, captain,
We must be neat—not neat, but cleanly, captain.
And yet the steer, the heifer, and the calf
Are all called neat.—Still virginalling
Upon his palm?—How now, you wanton calf—
Art thou my calf?

MAMILLIUS Yes, if you will, my lord.

LEONTES
Thou want'st a rough pash and the shoots that I have,
To be full like me. Yet they say we are
Almost as like as eggs. Women say so,
That will say anything. But were they false
As o'er-dyed blacks, as wind, as waters, false
As dice are to be wished by one that fixes
No bourn 'twixt his and mine, yet were it true
To say this boy were like me. Come, sir page,
Look on me with your welkin eye. Sweet villain,

Most dear'st, my collop! Can thy dam—may't be?—
Affection, thy intention stabs the centre.
Thou dost make possible things not so held,
Communicat'st with dreams—how can this be?—
With what's unreal thou coactive art,
And fellow'st nothing. Then 'tis very credent
Thou mayst co-join with something, and thou dost—
And that beyond commission; and I find it—
And that to the infection of my brains
And hard'ning of my brows.

POLIXENES What means Sicilia?

HERMIONE
He something seems unsettled.

POLIXENES How, my lord!

LEONTES
What cheer? How is't with you, best brother?

HERMIONE You look
As if you held a brow of much distraction.
Are you moved, my lord?

LEONTES No, in good earnest.
How sometimes nature will betray its folly,
Its tenderness, and make itself a pastime
To harder bosoms! Looking on the lines
Of my boy's face, methoughts I did recoil
Twenty-three years, and saw myself unbreeched,
In my green velvet coat; my dagger muzzled,
Lest it should bite its master, and so prove,
As ornament oft does, too dangerous.
How like, methought, I then was to this kernel,
This squash, this gentleman.—Mine honest friend,
Will you take eggs for money?

MAMILLIUS No, my lord, I'll fight.

LEONTES

You will? Why, happy man be's dole!—My brother,
Are you so fond of your young prince as we
Do seem to be of ours?

POLIXENES If at home, sir,
He's all my exercise, my mirth, my matter;
Now my sworn friend, and then mine enemy;
My parasite, my soldier, statesman, all.
He makes a July's day short as December,
And with his varying childness cures in me
Thoughts that would thick my blood.

LEONTES So stands this squire
Officed with me. We two will walk, my lord,
And leave you to your graver steps. Hermione,
How thou lov'st us show in our brother's welcome.
Let what is dear in Sicily be cheap.
Next to thyself and my young rover, he's
Apparent to my heart.

HERMIONE If you would seek us,
We are yours i'th' garden. Shall's attend you there?

LEONTES

To your own bents dispose you. You'll be found,
Be you beneath the sky. (*Aside*) I am angling now,
Though you perceive me not how I give line.
Go to, go to!
How she holds up the neb, the bill to him,
And arms her with the boldness of a wife
To her allowing husband!

Exeunt Polixenes and Hermione

Gone already.

Inch-thick, knee-deep, o'er head and ears a forked one!—
Go play, boy, play. Thy mother plays, and I
Play too; but so disgraced a part, whose issue
Will hiss me to my grave. Contempt and clamour
Will be my knell. Go play, boy, play. There have been,
Or I am much deceived, cuckolds ere now,
And many a man there is, even at this present,
Now, while I speak this, holds his wife by th'arm,
That little thinks she has been sluiced in 's absence,
And his pond fished by his next neighbour, by
Sir Smile, his neighbour. Nay, there's comfort in't,
Whiles other men have gates, and those gates opened,
As mine, against their will. Should all despair
That have revolted wives, the tenth of mankind
Would hang themselves. Physic for't there's none.
It is a bawdy planet, that will strike
Where 'tis predominant; and 'tis powerful. Think it:
From east, west, north, and south, be it concluded,
No barricado for a belly. Know't,
It will let in and out the enemy
With bag and baggage. Many thousand on's
Have the disease and feel't not.

Sir Ian McKellen played Macbeth and Leontes with the Royal Shakespeare Company in 1976.

PETER McENERY

✡

Julius Caesar

Act II Scene 1

Brutus mulls over the possible reasons for assassinating Julius Caesar.

It must be by his death. And for my part
I know no personal cause to spurn at him,
But for the general. He would be crowned.
How that might change his nature, there's the question.
It is the bright day that brings forth the adder,
And that craves wary walking. Crown him: that!
And then I grant we put a sting in him
That at his will he may do danger with.
Th'abuse of greatness is when it disjoins
Remorse from power. And to speak truth of Caesar,
I have not known when his affections swayed
More than his reason. But 'tis a common proof
That lowliness is young ambition's ladder,
Whereto the climber-upward turns his face;
But when he once attains the upmost round,
He then unto the ladder turns his back,
Looks in the clouds, scorning the base degrees
By which he did ascend. So Caesar may.
Then lest he may, prevent. And since the quarrel

Will bear no colour for the thing he is,
Fashion it thus: that what he is, augmented,
Would run to these and these extremities;
And therefore think him as a serpent's egg,
Which, hatched, would as his kind grow mischievous,
And kill him in the shell.

Troilus and Cressida

Act I Scene 3

Ulysses offers his explanation of the Greeks' ill success in the Siege of Troy.

ULYSSES

Troy, yet upon his basis, had been down
And the great Hector's sword had lacked a master
But for these instances:
The specialty of rule hath been neglected.
And look how many Grecian tents do stand
Hollow upon this plain: so many hollow factions.
When that the general is not like the hive
To whom the foragers shall all repair,
What honey is expected? Degree being vizarded,
Th' unworthiest shows as fairly in the mask.
The heavens themselves, the planets, and this centre
Observe degree, priority, and place,
Infixture, course, proportion, season, form,
Office and custom, in all line of order.
And therefore is the glorious planet Sol

In noble eminence enthroned and sphered
Amidst the other, whose med'cinable eye
Corrects the ill aspects of planets evil
And posts like the commandment of a king,
Sans check, to good and bad. But when the planets
In evil mixture to disorder wander,
What plagues and what portents, what mutiny?
What raging of the sea, shaking of earth?
Commotion in the winds, frights, changes, horrors
Divert and crack, rend and deracinate
The unity and married calm of states
Quite from their fixture. O when degree is shaked,
Which is the ladder to all high designs,
The enterprise is sick. How could communities,
Degrees in schools, and brotherhoods in cities,
Peaceful commerce from dividable shores,
The primogenity and due of birth,
Prerogative of age, crowns, sceptres, laurels,
But by degree stand in authentic place?
Take but degree away, untune that string,
And hark what discord follows. Each thing meets
In mere oppugnancy. The bounded waters
Should lift their bosoms higher than the shores
And make a sop of all this solid globe;
Strength should be lord of imbecility,
And the rude son should strike his father dead.
Force should be right—or rather, right and wrong,
Between whose endless jar justice resides,
Should lose their names, and so should justice too.
Then everything includes itself in power,
Power into will, will into appetite;

And appetite, an universal wolf,
So doubly seconded with will and power,
Must make perforce an universal prey,
And last eat up himself. Great Agamemnon,
This chaos, when degree is suffocate,
Follows the choking.
And this neglection of degree it is
That by a pace goes backward in a purpose
It hath to climb. The general's disdained
By him one step below; he, by the next;
That next, by him beneath. So every step,
Exampled by the first pace that is sick
Of his superior, grows to an envious fever
Of pale and bloodless emulation.
And 'tis this fever that keeps Troy on foot,
Not her own sinews. To end a tale of length:
Troy in our weakness lives, not in her strength.

Peter McEnery played Brutus with the Royal Shakespeare Company in 1983.

HELEN MIRREN

☆

Hamlet

Act V Scene 2

Hamlet is about to fight a duel with Laertes, whose father, Polonius, he has killed.

HORATIO If your mind dislike anything, obey it. I will forestall their repair hither, and say you are not fit.

HAMLET Not a whit. We defy augury. There's a special providence in the fall of a sparrow. If it be now, 'tis not to come. If it be not to come, it will be now. If it be not now, yet it will come. The readiness is all. Since no man has aught of what he leaves, what is't to leave betimes?

Measure for Measure

Act II Scene 2

The novice Isabella comes to Angelo, Deputy to the Duke of Vienna, to plead for the life of her brother Claudio, condemned to die for fornication.

ANGELO ... You're welcome. What's your will?

ISABELLA

I am a woeful suitor to your honour.

Please but your honour hear me.

ANGELO Well, what's your suit?

ISABELLA

There is a vice that most I do abhor,
And most desire should meet the blow of justice,
For which I would not plead, but that I must;
For which I must not plead, but that I am
At war 'twixt will and will not.

ANGELO Well, the matter?

ISABELLA

I have a brother is condemned to die.
I do beseech you, let it be his fault,
And not my brother.

PROVOST (*aside*) Heaven give thee moving graces!

ANGELO

Condemn the fault, and not the actor of it?
Why, every fault's condemned ere it be done.
Mine were the very cipher of a function,
To fine the faults whose fine stands in record,
And let go by the actor.

ISABELLA O just but severe law!
I had a brother, then. Heaven keep your honour.

LUCIO (*aside to Isabella*)

Give't not o'er so. To him again; entreat him.
Kneel down before him; hang upon his gown.
You are too cold. If you should need a pin,
You could not with more tame a tongue desire it.
To him, I say!

ISABELLA (*to Angelo*) Must he needs die?

ANGELO Maiden, no remedy.

ISABELLA

Yes, I do think that you might pardon him,

And neither heaven nor man grieve at the mercy.
ANGELO I will not do't.
ISABELLA But can you if you would?
ANGELO
Look what I will not, that I cannot do.
ISABELLA
But might you do't, and do the world no wrong,
If so your heart were touched with that remorse
As mine is to him?
ANGELO He's sentenced; 'tis too late.
LUCIO (*aside to Isabella*) You are too cold.
ISABELLA
Too late? Why, no; I that do speak a word
May call it again. Well, believe this,
No ceremony that to great ones 'longs,
Not the king's crown, nor the deputed sword,
The marshal's truncheon, nor the judge's robe,
Become them with one half so good a grace
As mercy does.
If he had been as you and you as he,
You would have slipped like him, but he, like you,
Would not have been so stern.
ANGELO Pray you be gone.
ISABELLA
I would to heaven I had your potency,
And you were Isabel! Should it then be thus?
No; I would tell what 'twere to be a judge,
And what a prisoner.
LUCIO (*aside to Isabella*) Ay, touch him; there's the vein.
ANGELO
Your brother is a forfeit of the law,
And you but waste your words.

ISABELLA Alas, alas!
Why, all the souls that were were forfeit once,
And He that might the vantage best have took
Found out the remedy. How would you be
If He which is the top of judgement should
But judge you as you are? O, think on that,
And mercy then will breathe within your lips,
Like man new made.

ANGELO Be you content, fair maid.
It is the law, not I, condemn your brother.
Were he my kinsman, brother, or my son,
It should be thus with him. He must die tomorrow.

ISABELLA
Tomorrow? O, that's sudden! Spare him, spare him!
He's not prepared for death. Even for our kitchens
We kill the fowl of season. Shall we serve heaven
With less respect than we do minister
To our gross selves? Good good my lord, bethink you:
Who is it that hath died for this offence?
There's many have committed it.

LUCIO (*aside*) Ay, well said.

ANGELO
The law hath not been dead, though it hath slept.
Those many had not dared to do that evil
If the first that did th'edict infringe
Had answered for his deed. Now 'tis awake,
Takes note of what is done, and, like a prophet,
Looks in a glass that shows what future evils,
Either raw, or by remissness new conceived
And so in progress to be hatched and born,
Are now to have no successive degrees,

But ere they live, to end.

ISABELLA Yet show some pity.

ANGELO

I show it most of all when I show justice,
For then I pity those I do not know
Which a dismissed offence would after gall,
And do him right that, answering one foul wrong,
Lives not to act another. Be satisfied.
Your brother dies tomorrow. Be content.

ISABELLA

So you must be the first that gives this sentence,
And he that suffers. O, it is excellent
To have a giant's strength, but it is tyrannous
To use it like a giant.

LUCIO (*aside to Isabella*) That's well said.

ISABELLA Could great men thunder
As Jove himself does, Jove would never be quiet,
For every pelting petty officer
Would use his heaven for thunder, nothing but thunder.
Merciful heaven,
Thou rather with thy sharp and sulphurous bolt
Split'st the unwedgeable and gnarlèd oak
Than the soft myrtle. But man, proud man,
Dressed in a little brief authority,
Most ignorant of what he's most assured,
His glassy essence, like an angry ape
Plays such fantastic tricks before high heaven
As makes the angels weep, who, with our spleens,
Would all themselves laugh mortal.

LUCIO (*aside to Isabella*)

O, to him, to him, wench! He will relent.

He's coming; I perceive't.
PROVOST (*aside*) Pray heaven she win him!
ISABELLA
We cannot weigh our brother with ourself.
Great men may jest with saints; 'tis wit in them,
But in the less, foul profanation.
LUCIO (*aside to Isabella*) Thou'rt i'th' right, girl. More o'that.
ISABELLA
That in the captain's but a choleric word,
Which in the soldier is flat blasphemy.
LUCIO (*aside to Isabella*) Art advised o' that? More on't.
ANGELO
Why do you put these sayings upon me?
ISABELLA
Because authority, though it err like others,
Hath yet a kind of medicine in itself
That skins the vice o'th' top. Go to your bosom;
Knock there, and ask your heart what it doth know
That's like my brother's fault. If it confess
A natural guiltiness, such as is his,
Let it not sound a thought upon your tongue
Against my brother's life.
ANGELO (*aside*) She speaks, and 'tis such sense
That my sense breeds with it.
(*To Isabella*) Fare you well.
ISABELLA Gentle my lord, turn back.
ANGELO
I will bethink me. Come again tomorrow.
ISABELLA
Hark how I'll bribe you; good my lord, turn back.
ANGELO How, bribe me?

ISABELLA
Ay, with such gifts that heaven shall share with you.
LUCIO (*aside to Isabella*) You had marred all else.
ISABELLA
Not with fond shekels of the tested gold,
Or stones, whose rate are either rich or poor
As fancy values them; but with true prayers,
That shall be up at heaven and enter there
Ere sunrise, prayers from preservèd souls,
From fasting maids whose minds are dedicate
To nothing temporal.
ANGELO Well, come to me tomorrow.
LUCIO (*aside to Isabella*) Go to; 'tis well; away.
ISABELLA Heaven keep your honour safe.
ANGELO (*aside*) Amen;
For I am that way going to temptation,
Where prayer is crossed.
ISABELLA At what hour tomorrow
Shall I attend your lordship?
ANGELO At any time fore noon.
ISABELLA God save your honour.
ANGELO (*aside*) From thee; even from thy virtue.

Helen Mirren, whose roles with the Royal Shakespeare Company include Ophelia, Lady Macbeth, and Cleopatra, played Isabella at the Riverside Studios in 1979.

CHERRY MORRIS

✡

The Comedy of Errors

Act V Scene 1

Antipholus of Syracuse, supposed to be mad, has taken refuge in a priory from Adriana, wife of his long-lost twin brother.

Enter from the priory the Lady Abbess

ABBESS
Be quiet, people. Wherefore throng you hither?

ADRIANA
To fetch my poor distracted husband hence.
Let us come in, that we may bind him fast,
And bear him home for his recovery.

ANGELO
I knew he was not in his perfect wits.

SECOND MERCHANT
I am sorry now that I did draw on him.

ABBESS
How long hath this possession held the man?

ADRIANA
This week he hath been heavy, sour, sad,
And much, much different from the man he was;
But till this afternoon his passion
Ne'er brake into extremity of rage.

ABBESS
Hath he not lost much wealth by wreck at sea?
Buried some dear friend? Hath not else his eye
Strayed his affection in unlawful love—
A sin prevailing much in youthful men,
Who give their eyes the liberty of gazing?
Which of these sorrows is he subject to?

ADRIANA
To none of these, except it be the last,
Namely some love that drew him oft from home.

ABBESS
You should for that have reprehended him.

ADRIANA Why, so I did.

ABBESS Ay, but not rough enough.

ADRIANA
As roughly as my modesty would let me.

ABBESS Haply in private.

ADRIANA And in assemblies too.

ABBESS Ay, but not enough.

ADRIANA
It was the copy of our conference.
In bed he slept not for my urging it.
At board he fed not for my urging it.
Alone, it was the subject of my theme.
In company I often glancèd it.
Still did I tell him it was vile and bad.

ABBESS
And thereof came it that the man was mad.
The venom clamours of a jealous woman
Poisons more deadly than a mad dog's tooth.
It seems his sleeps were hindered by thy railing,

And thereof comes it that his head is light.
Thou sayst his meat was sauced with thy upbraidings.
Unquiet meals make ill digestions.
Thereof the raging fire of fever bred,
And what's a fever but a fit of madness?
Thou sayst his sports were hindered by thy brawls.
Sweet recreation barred, what doth ensue
But moody and dull melancholy,
Kinsman to grim and comfortless despair,
And at her heels a huge infectious troop
Of pale distemperatures and foes to life?
In food, in sport, and life-preserving rest
To be disturbed would mad or man or beast.
The consequence is, then, thy jealous fits
Hath scared thy husband from the use of wits.

Cherry Morris played the Abbess with the Royal Shakespeare Company in 1990.

JOHN NETTLES

✡

The Winter's Tale

Act V Scene 3

Paulina has brought about Leontes' reunion with his wife Hermione, whom he had believed dead.

LEONTES O peace, Paulina!
Thou shouldst a husband take by my consent,
As I by thine a wife. This is a match,
And made between's by vows. Thou hast found mine,
But how is to be questioned, for I saw her,
As I thought, dead, and have in vain said many
A prayer upon her grave. I'll not seek far—
For him, I partly know his mind—to find thee
An honourable husband. Come, Camillo,
And take her by the hand, whose worth and honesty
Is richly noted, and here justified
By us, a pair of kings. Let's from this place.
(*To Hermione*) What, look upon my brother. Both your
pardons,
That e'er I put between your holy looks
My ill suspicion. This' your son-in-law
And son unto the King, whom heavens directing
Is troth-plight to your daughter. Good Paulina,

Lead us from hence, where we may leisurely
Each one demand and answer to his part
Performed in this wide gap of time since first
We were dissevered. Hastily lead away.

John Nettles played Leontes with the Royal Shakespeare Company in 1992.

RICHARD PASCO

✡

Richard II

Act III Scene 2

King Richard, deposed by Bolingbroke, laments his fate.

AUMERLE

Where is the Duke my father, with his power?

KING RICHARD

No matter where. Of comfort no man speak.
Let's talk of graves, of worms and epitaphs,
Make dust our paper, and with rainy eyes
Write sorrow on the bosom of the earth.
Let's choose executors and talk of wills—
And yet not so, for what can we bequeath
Save our deposèd bodies to the ground?
Our lands, our lives, and all are Bolingbroke's;
And nothing can we call our own but death,
And that small model of the barren earth
Which serves as paste and cover to our bones.
For God's sake, let us sit upon the ground,
And tell sad stories of the death of kings—
How some have been deposed, some slain in war,
Some haunted by the ghosts they have deposed,
Some poisoned by their wives, some sleeping killed,

All murdered. For within the hollow crown
That rounds the mortal temples of a king
Keeps Death his court; and there the antic sits,
Scoffing his state and grinning at his pomp,
Allowing him a breath, a little scene,
To monarchize, be feared, and kill with looks,
Infusing him with self and vain conceit,
As if this flesh which walls about our life
Were brass impregnable; and humoured thus,
Comes at the last, and with a little pin
Bores through his castle wall; and farewell, king.
Cover your heads, and mock not flesh and blood
With solemn reverence. Throw away respect,
Tradition, form, and ceremonious duty,
For you have but mistook me all this while.
I live with bread, like you; feel want,
Taste grief, need friends. Subjected thus,
How can you say to me I am a king?

BISHOP OF CARLISLE

My lord, wise men ne'er wail their present woes,
But presently prevent the ways to wail.
To fear the foe, since fear oppresseth strength,
Gives in your weakness strength unto your foe;
And so your follies fight against yourself.
Fear, and be slain. No worse can come to fight;
And fight and die is death destroying death,
Where fearing dying pays death servile breath.

Timon of Athens

Act V Scene 2

Exiled from Athens, Timon prepares for death.

Come not to me again, but say to Athens,
Timon hath made his everlasting mansion
Upon the beachèd verge of the salt flood,
Who once a day with his embossèd froth
The turbulent surge shall cover. Thither come,
And let my gravestone be your oracle.
Lips, let four words go by, and language end.
What is amiss, plague and infection mend.
Graves only be men's works, and death their gain.
Sun, hide thy beams. Timon hath done his reign.

Exit into his cave

Richard Pasco played Richard II with the Royal Shakespeare Company in 1973, and Timon in 1980.

JOANNE PEARCE

✡

Cymbeline

Act I Scene 3

Imogen questions her husband Posthumus' servant about his master's departure from Milford Haven for Italy.

IMOGEN
I would thou grew'st unto the shores o'th' haven
And questionedst every sail. If he should write
And I not have it, 'twere a paper lost
As offered mercy is. What was the last
That he spake to thee?
PISANIO It was his queen, his queen.
IMOGEN Then waved his handkerchief?
PISANIO And kissed it, madam.
IMOGEN Senseless linen, happier therein than I!
And that was all?
PISANIO No, madam. For so long
As he could make me with this eye or ear
Distinguish him from others he did keep
The deck, with glove or hat or handkerchief
Still waving, as the fits and stirs of 's mind
Could best express how slow his soul sailed on,
How swift his ship.

IMOGEN Thou shouldst have made him
As little as a crow, or less, ere left
To after-eye him.
PISANIO Madam, so I did.
IMOGEN
I would have broke mine eye-strings, cracked them, but
To look upon him till the diminution
Of space had pointed him sharp as my needle;
Nay, followed him till he had melted from
The smallness of a gnat to air, and then
Have turned mine eye and wept. But, good Pisanio,
When shall we hear from him?
PISANIO Be assured, madam,
With his next vantage.
IMOGEN
I did not take my leave of him, but had
Most pretty things to say. Ere I could tell him
How I would think on him at certain hours,
Such thoughts and such, or I could make him swear
The shes of Italy should not betray
Mine interest and his honour, or have charged him
At the sixth hour of morn, at noon, at midnight
T'encounter me with orisons—for then
I am in heaven for him—or ere I could
Give him that parting kiss which I had set
Betwixt two charming words, comes in my father,
And, like the tyrannous breathing of the north,
Shakes all our buds from growing.

Joanne Pearce played Imogen with the Royal Shakespeare Company in 1997.

MICHAEL PENNINGTON

☆

Romeo and Juliet

Act I Scene 4

Mercutio tells Romeo of his dream of Queen Mab.

ROMEO I dreamt a dream tonight.
MERCUTIO And so did I.
ROMEO Well, what was yours?
MERCUTIO That dreamers often lie.
ROMEO
In bed asleep while they do dream things true.
MERCUTIO
O, then I see Queen Mab hath been with you.
BENVOLIO Queen Mab, what's she?
MERCUTIO
She is the fairies' midwife, and she comes
In shape no bigger than an agate stone
On the forefinger of an alderman,
Drawn with a team of little atomi
Athwart men's noses as they lie asleep.
Her wagon spokes made of long spinners' legs;
The cover, of the wings of grasshoppers;
Her traces, of the moonshine's wat'ry beams;
Her collars, of the smallest spider web;
Her whip, of cricket's bone, the lash of film;

Her wagoner, a small grey-coated gnat
Not half so big as a round little worm
Pricked from the lazy finger of a maid.
Her chariot is an empty hazelnut
Made by the joiner squirrel or old grub,
Time out o' mind the fairies' coachmakers.
And in this state she gallops night by night
Through lovers' brains, and then they dream of love;
O'er courtiers' knees, that dream on curtsies straight;
O'er ladies' lips, who straight on kisses dream,
Which oft the angry Mab with blisters plagues
Because their breaths with sweetmeats tainted are.
Sometime she gallops o'er a lawyer's lip,
And then dreams he of smelling out a suit;
And sometime comes she with a tithe-pig's tail
Tickling a parson's nose as a lies asleep;
Then dreams he of another benefice.
Sometime she driveth o'er a soldier's neck,
And then dreams he of cutting foreign throats,
Of breaches, ambuscados, Spanish blades,
Of healths five fathom deep; and then anon
Drums in his ear, at which he starts and wakes,
And being thus frighted, swears a prayer or two,
And sleeps again. This is that very Mab
That plaits the manes of horses in the night,
And bakes the elf-locks in foul sluttish hairs,
Which once untangled much misfortune bodes.
This is the hag, when maids lie on their backs,
That presses them and learns them first to bear,
Making them women of good carriage.
This is she—

ROMEO Peace, peace, Mercutio, peace!

Thou talk'st of nothing.
MERCUTIO True. I talk of dreams,
Which are the children of an idle brain,
Begot of nothing but vain fantasy,
Which is as thin of substance as the air,
And more inconstant than the wind, who woos
Even now the frozen bosom of the north,
And, being angered, puffs away from thence,
Turning his face to the dew-dropping south.

Michael Pennington played Mercutio with the Royal Shakespeare Company in 1976

EDWARD PETHERBRIDGE

✡

Love's Labour's Lost

Act I Scene 2

Don Armado is in love with the country wench Jaquenetta.

ARMADO I do affect the very ground—which is base—where her shoe—which is baser—guided by her foot—which is basest—doth tread. I shall be forsworn—which is a great argument of falsehood—if I love. And how can that be true love which is falsely attempted? Love is a familiar; love is a devil. There is no evil angel but love. Yet was Samson so tempted, and he had an excellent strength. Yet was Solomon so seduced, and he had a very good wit. Cupid's butt-shaft is too hard for Hercules' club, and therefore too much odds for a Spaniard's rapier. The first and second cause will not serve my turn: the passado he respects not, the duello he regards not. His disgrace is to be called boy, but his glory is to subdue men. Adieu, valour; rust, rapier; be still, drum: for your manager is in love; yea, he loveth. Assist me, some extemporal god of rhyme, for I am sure I shall turn sonnet. Devise wit, write pen, for I am for whole volumes, in folio. *Exit*

Edward Petherbridge played Don Armado with the Royal Shakespeare Company in 1984.

JONATHAN PRYCE

✡

Macbeth

Act V Scene 5

Macbeth, buoyed up by the Witches' false prophecies, heras that his wife has died.

Enter Macbeth, Seyton, and soldiers, with a drummer and colours

MACBETH

Hang out our banners on the outward walls.
The cry is still 'They come.' Our castle's strength
Will laugh a siege to scorn. Here let them lie
Till famine and the ague eat them up.
Were they not forced with those that should be ours
We might have met them dareful, beard to beard,
And beat them backward home.

A cry within of women

What is that noise?

SEYTON It is the cry of women, my good lord. *Exit*

MACBETH

I have almost forgot the taste of fears.
The time has been my senses would have cooled
To hear a night-shriek, and my fell of hair
Would at a dismal treatise rouse and stir
As life were in't. I have supped full with horrors.

Direness, familiar to my slaughterous thoughts,
Cannot once start me.

Enter Seyton

Wherefore was that cry?

SEYTON The Queen, my lord, is dead.

MACBETH She should have died hereafter.
There would have been a time for such a word.
Tomorrow, and tomorrow, and tomorrow
Creeps in this petty pace from day to day
To the last syllable of recorded time,
And all our yesterdays have lighted fools
The way to dusty death. Out, out, brief candle.
Life's but a walking shadow, a poor player
That struts and frets his hour upon the stage,
And then is heard no more. It is a tale
Told by an idiot, full of sound and fury,
Signifying nothing.

Enter a Messenger

Thou com'st to use
Thy tongue: thy story quickly.

MESSENGER Gracious my lord,
I should report that which I say I saw,
But know not how to do't.

MACBETH Well, say, sir.

MESSENGER
As I did stand my watch upon the hill
I looked toward Birnam, and anon methought
The wood began to move.

MACBETH Liar and slave!

MESSENGER
Let me endure your wrath if't be not so.
Within this three mile may you see it coming.

I say, a moving grove.

MACBETH If thou speak'st false
Upon the next tree shall thou hang alive
Till famine cling thee. If thy speech be sooth,
I care not if thou dost for me as much.
I pall in resolution, and begin
To doubt th' equivocation of the fiend,
That lies like truth. 'Fear not till Birnam Wood
Do come to Dunsinane'—and now a wood
Comes toward Dunsinane. Arm, arm, and out.
If this which he avouches does appear
There is nor flying hence nor tarrying here.
I 'gin to be aweary of the sun,
And wish th' estate o'th' world were now undone.
Ring the alarum bell. (*Alarums*) Blow wind, come wrack,
At least we'll die with harness on our back.

Exeunt

Jonathan Pryce played Macbeth with the Royal Shakespeare Company in 1986.

ROGER REES

✡

Cymbeline

Act II Scene 5

Posthumus believes himself betrayed by Imogen with Iachimo.

Is there no way for men to be, but women
Must be half-workers? We are bastards all,
And that most venerable man which I
Did call my father was I know not where
When I was stamped. Some coiner with his tools
Made me a counterfeit; yet my mother seemed
The Dian of that time: so doth my wife
The nonpareil of this. O vengeance, vengeance!
Me of my lawful pleasure she restrained,
And prayed me oft forbearance; did it with
A pudency so rosy the sweet view on't
Might well have warmed old Saturn; that I thought her
As chaste as unsunned snow. O all the devils!
This yellow Iachimo in an hour—was't not?—
Or less—at first? Perchance he spoke not, but
Like a full-acorned boar, a German one,
Cried 'O!' and mounted; found no opposition
But what he looked for should oppose and she
Should from encounter guard. Could I find out

The woman's part in me—for there's no motion
That tends to vice in man but I affirm
It is the woman's part; be it lying, note it,
The woman's; flattering, hers; deceiving, hers;
Lust and rank thoughts, hers, hers; revenges, hers;
Ambitions, covetings, change of prides, disdain,
Nice longing, slanders, mutability,
All faults that man can name, nay, that hell knows,
Why, hers in part or all, but rather all—
For even to vice
They are not constant, but are changing still
One vice but of a minute old for one
Not half so old as that. I'll write against them,
Detest them, curse them, yet 'tis greater skill
In a true hate to pray they have their will.
The very devils cannot plague them better.

Roger Rees played Posthumus with the Royal Shakespeare Company in 1979.

IAN RICHARDSON

✡

Love's Labour's Lost

Act IV Scene 3

The King of Navarre and his friends have discovered that, in spite of their vows to withdraw from the world, they have all fallen in love.

KING
But what of this? Are we not all in love?
BEROWNE
Nothing so sure, and thereby all forsworn.
KING
Then leave this chat and, good Berowne, now prove
Our loving lawful and our faith not torn.
DUMAINE
Ay, marry there, some flattery for this evil.
LONGUEVILLE
O, some authority how to proceed,
Some tricks, some quillets how to cheat the devil.
DUMAINE
Some salve for perjury.
BEROWNE O, 'tis more than need.
Have at you, then, affection's men-at-arms.
Consider what you first did swear unto:
To fast, to study, and to see no woman—

Flat treason 'gainst the kingly state of youth.
Say, can you fast? Your stomachs are too young,
And abstinence engenders maladies.
O, we have made a vow to study, lords,
And in that vow we have forsworn our books;
For when would you, my liege, or you, or you
In leaden contemplation have found out
Such fiery numbers as the prompting eyes
Of beauty's tutors have enriched you with?
Other slow arts entirely keep the brain,
And therefore, finding barren practisers,
Scarce show a harvest of their heavy toil.
But love, first learnèd in a lady's eyes,
Lives not alone immurèd in the brain,
But with the motion of all elements
Courses as swift as thought in every power,
And gives to every power a double power
Above their functions and their offices.
It adds a precious seeing to the eye—
A lover's eyes will gaze an eagle blind.
A lover's ear will hear the lowest sound
When the suspicious head of theft is stopped.
Love's feeling is more soft and sensible
Than are the tender horns of cockled snails.
Love's tongue proves dainty Bacchus gross in taste.
For valour, is not love a Hercules,
Still climbing trees in the Hesperides?
Subtle as Sphinx, as sweet and musical
As bright Apollo's lute strung with his hair;
And when love speaks, the voice of all the gods
Make heaven drowsy with the harmony.

Never durst poet touch a pen to write
Until his ink were tempered with love's sighs.
O, then his lines would ravish savage ears,
And plant in tyrants mild humility.
From women's eyes this doctrine I derive.
They sparkle still the right Promethean fire.
They are the books, the arts, the academes
That show, contain, and nourish all the world,
Else none at all in aught proves excellent.
Then fools you were these women to forswear,
Or keeping what is sworn, you will prove fools.
For wisdom's sake—a word that all men love—
Or for love's sake—a word that loves all men—
Or for men's sake—the authors of these women—
Or women's sake—by whom we men are men—
Let us once lose our oaths to find ourselves,
Or else we lose ourselves to keep our oaths.
It is religion to be thus forsworn,
For charity itself fulfils the law,
And who can sever love from charity?

Ian Richardson played Berowne with the Royal Shakespeare Company in 1973.

PAUL SCOFIELD

☆

King Lear

Act III Scene 4

Lear, rejected by the daughters in whom he had placed his hope, endures storm and tempest in the company of his faithful fool and the loyal Earl of Kent.

LEAR

Thou think'st 'tis much that this contentious storm
Invades us to the skin. So 'tis to thee;
But where the greater malady is fixed,
The lesser is scarce felt. Thou'dst shun a bear,
But if thy flight lay toward the roaring sea
Thou'dst meet the bear i'th' mouth. When the mind's free,
The body's delicate. This tempest in my mind
Doth from my senses take all feeling else
Save what beats there: filial ingratitude.
Is it not as this mouth should tear this hand
For lifting food to't? But I will punish home.
No, I will weep no more.—In such a night
To shut me out? Pour on, I will endure.
In such a night as this! O Regan, Goneril,
Your old kind father, whose frank heart gave all—
O, that way madness lies. Let me shun that.

No more of that.

KENT Good my lord, enter here.

LEAR

Prithee, go in thyself. Seek thine own ease.
This tempest will not give me leave to ponder
On things would hurt me more; but I'll go in.
(*To his Fool*) In, boy; go first.

He kneels

You houseless poverty—
Nay, get thee in. I'll pray, and then I'll sleep.

Exit Fool

Poor naked wretches, wheresoe'er you are,
That bide the pelting of this pitiless storm,
How shall your houseless heads and unfed sides,
Your looped and windowed raggedness, defend you
From seasons such as these? O, I have ta'en
Too little care of this. Take physic, pomp,
Expose thyself to feel what wretches feel,
That thou mayst shake the superflux to them
And show the heavens more just.

The Tempest

Act V Scene 1

Prospero, whose enemies are now within his power, renounces his magic.

Prospero draws a circle with his staff

PROSPERO

Ye elves of hills, brooks, standing lakes and groves,
And ye that on the sands with printless foot
Do chase the ebbing Neptune, and do fly him
When he comes back; you demi-puppets that
By moonshine do the green sour ringlets make
Whereof the ewe not bites; and you whose pastime
Is to make midnight mushrooms, that rejoice
To hear the solemn curfew; by whose aid,
Weak masters though ye be, I have bedimmed
The noontide sun, called forth the mutinous winds,
And 'twixt the green sea and the azured vault
Set roaring war—to the dread rattling thunder
Have I given fire, and rifted Jove's stout oak
With his own bolt; the strong-based promontory
Have I made shake, and by the spurs plucked up
The pine and cedar; graves at my command
Have waked their sleepers, oped, and let 'em forth
By my so potent art. But this rough magic
I here abjure. And when I have required
Some heavenly music—which even now I do—
To work mine end upon their senses that
This airy charm is for, I'll break my staff,

Bury it certain fathoms in the earth,
And deeper than did ever plummet sound
I'll drown my book.

Paul Scofield played Lear with the Royal Shakespeare Company in 1964 and Prospero at the Leeds Playhouse and Wyndham's Theatre, London, in 1974.

ANTONY SHER

✡

The Merchant of Venice

Act IV Scene 1

Shylock has come before the Duke of Venice to demand his pound of flesh from Antonio.

DUKE . . .
Shylock, the world thinks—and I think so too—
That thou but lead'st this fashion of thy malice
To the last hour of act, and then 'tis thought
Thou'lt show thy mercy and remorse more strange
Than is thy strange apparent cruelty,
And where thou now exacts the penalty—
Which is a pound of this poor merchant's flesh—
Thou wilt not only loose the forfeiture,
But, touched with human gentleness and love,
Forgive a moiety of the principal,
Glancing an eye of pity on his losses,
That have of late so huddled on his back
Enough to press a royal merchant down
And pluck commiseration of his state
From brassy bosoms and rough hearts of flint,
From stubborn Turks and Tartars never trained
To offices of tender courtesy.
We all expect a gentle answer, Jew.

SHYLOCK

I have possessed your grace of what I purpose,
And by our holy Sabbath have I sworn
To have the due and forfeit of my bond.
If you deny it, let the danger light
Upon your charter and your city's freedom.
You'll ask me why I rather choose to have
A weight of carrion flesh than to receive
Three thousand ducats. I'll not answer that,
But say it is my humour. Is it answered?
What if my house be troubled with a rat,
And I be pleased to give ten thousand ducats
To have it baned? What, are you answered yet?
Some men there are love not a gaping pig,
Some that are mad if they behold a cat,
And others when the bagpipe sings i'th' nose
Cannot contain their urine; for affection,
Mistress of passion, sways it to the mood
Of what it likes or loathes. Now for your answer:
As there is no firm reason to be rendered
Why he cannot abide a gaping pig,
Why he a harmless necessary cat,
Why he a woollen bagpipe, but of force
Must yield to such inevitable shame
As to offend himself being offended,
So can I give no reason, nor I will not,
More than a lodged hate and a certain loathing
I bear Antonio, that I follow thus
A losing suit against him. Are you answered?

BASSANIO

This is no answer, thou unfeeling man,
To excuse the current of thy cruelty.

SHYLOCK

I am not bound to please thee with my answers.

BASSANIO

Do all men kill the things they do not love?

SHYLOCK

Hates any man the thing he would not kill?

BASSANIO

Every offence is not a hate at first.

SHYLOCK

What, wouldst thou have a serpent sting thee twice?

ANTONIO

I pray you think you question with the Jew.
You may as well go stand upon the beach
And bid the main flood bate his usual height;
You may as well use question with the wolf
Why he hath made the ewe bleat for the lamb;
You may as well forbid the mountain pines
To wag their high tops and to make no noise
When they are fretten with the gusts of heaven,
You may as well do anything most hard
As seek to soften that—than which what's harder?—
His Jewish heart. Therefore, I do beseech you,
Make no more offers, use no farther means,
But with all brief and plain conveniency
Let me have judgement and the Jew his will.

BASSANIO

For thy three thousand ducats here is six.

SHYLOCK

If every ducat in six thousand ducats
Were in six parts, and every part a ducat,
I would not draw them. I would have my bond.

DUKE

How shalt thou hope for mercy, rend'ring none?

SHYLOCK

What judgement shall I dread, doing no wrong?
You have among you many a purchased slave
Which, like your asses and your dogs and mules,
You use in abject and in slavish parts
Because you bought them. Shall I say to you
'Let them be free, marry them to your heirs.
Why sweat they under burdens? Let their beds
Be made as soft as yours, and let their palates
Be seasoned with such viands.' You will answer
'The slaves are ours.' So do I answer you.
The pound of flesh which I demand of him
Is dearly bought. 'Tis mine, and I will have it.
If you deny me, fie upon your law:
There is no force in the decrees of Venice.
I stand for judgement. Answer: shall I have it?

Antony Sher played Shylock with the Royal Shakespeare Company in 1987.

DONALD SINDEN

✡

Titus Andronicus

Act V Scene 2

Titus takes his revenge on Chiron and Demetrius, who ravished and mutilated his daughter Lavinia.

Enter Titus Andronicus with a knife, and Lavinia with a basin

TITUS

Come, come, Lavinia. Look, thy foes are bound.
Sirs, stop their mouths. Let them not speak to me,
But let them hear what fearful words I utter.
O villains, Chiron and Demetrius!
Here stands the spring whom you have stained with mud,
This goodly summer with your winter mixed.
You killed her husband, and for that vile fault
Two of her brothers were condemned to death,
My hand cut off and made a merry jest,
Both her sweet hands, her tongue, and that more dear
Than hands or tongue, her spotless chastity,
Inhuman traitors, you constrained and forced.
What would you say if I should let you speak?
Villains, for shame. You could not beg for grace.
Hark, wretches, how I mean to martyr you.

This one hand yet is left to cut your throats,
Whiles that Lavinia 'tween her stumps doth hold
The basin that receives your guilty blood.
You know your mother means to feast with me,
And calls herself Revenge, and thinks me mad.
Hark, villains, I will grind your bones to dust,
And with your blood and it I'll make a paste,
And of the paste a coffin I will rear,
And make two pasties of your shameful heads,
And bid that strumpet, your unhallowed dam,
Like to the earth swallow her own increase.
This is the feast that I have bid her to,
And this the banquet she shall surfeit on;
For worse than Philomel you used my daughter,
And worse than Progne I will be revenged.
And now, prepare your throats. Lavinia, come.
Receive the blood, and when that they are dead
Let me go grind their bones to powder small,
And with this hateful liquor temper it,
And in that paste let their vile heads be baked.
Come, come, be everyone officious
To make this banquet, which I wish may prove
More stern and bloody than the Centaurs' feast.
He cuts their throats
So, now bring them in, for I'll play the cook
And see them ready against their mother comes.

Twelfth Night

Act II Scene 4

The love-sick Duke Orsino seeks consolation in music and the company of his page Cesario – actually Viola, who has fallen in love with him.

ORSINO
Give me some music. Now good morrow, friends.
Now good Cesario, but that piece of song,
That old and antic song we heard last night.
Methought it did relieve my passion much,
More than light airs and recollected terms
Of these most brisk and giddy-pacèd times.
Come, but one verse.

CURIO
He is not here, so please your lordship, that should sing it.

ORSINO Who was it?

CURIO Feste the jester, my lord, a fool that the lady Olivia's father took much delight in. He is about the house.

ORSINO
Seek him out, and play the tune the while.

Exit Curio

Music plays

Come hither, boy. If ever thou shalt love,
In the sweet pangs of it remember me;
For such as I am, all true lovers are,
Unstaid and skittish in all motions else
Save in the constant image of the creature
That is beloved. How dost thou like this tune?

VIOLA
It gives a very echo to the seat
Where love is throned.
ORSINO Thou dost speak masterly.
My life upon't, young though thou art thine eye
Hath stayed upon some favour that it loves.
Hath it not, boy?
VIOLA A little, by your favour.
ORSINO What kind of woman is't?
VIOLA Of your complexion.
ORSINO
She is not worth thee then. What years, i'faith?
VIOLA
About your years, my lord.
ORSINO
Too old, by heaven. Let still the woman take
An elder than herself. So wears she to him;
So sways she level in her husband's heart.
For, boy, however we do praise ourselves,
Our fancies are more giddy and unfirm,
More longing, wavering, sooner lost and worn,
Than women's are.
VIOLA I think it well, my lord.
ORSINO
Then let thy love be younger than thyself,
Or thy affection cannot hold the bent;
For women are as roses, whose fair flower
Being once displayed, doth fall that very hour.
VIOLA
And so they are. Alas that they are so:
To die even when they to perfection grow.

Enter Curio and Feste the clown

ORSINO

O fellow, come, the song we had last night.
Mark it, Cesario, it is old and plain.
The spinners, and the knitters in the sun,
And the free maids that weave their thread with bones,
Do use to chant it. It is silly sooth,
And dallies with the innocence of love,
Like the old age.

Donald Sinden's many roles with the Royal Shakespeare Company include Othello, Lear, Benedick, Malvolio and Henry VIII.

ELIZABETH SPRIGGS

✡

Much Ado About Nothing

Act II Scene 1

Beatrice lacks a suitor.

DON PEDRO In faith, lady, you have a merry heart.

BEATRICE Yea, my lord, I thank it. Poor fool, it keeps on the windy side of care.—My cousin tells him in his ear that he is in her heart.

CLAUDIO And so she doth, cousin.

BEATRICE Good Lord, for alliance! Thus goes everyone to the world but I, and I am sunburnt. I may sit in a corner and cry 'Heigh-ho for a husband'.

DON PEDRO Lady Beatrice, I will get you one.

BEATRICE I would rather have one of your father's getting. Hath your grace ne'er a brother like you? Your father got excellent husbands if a maid could come by them.

DON PEDRO Will you have me, lady?

BEATRICE No, my lord, unless I might have another for working days. Your grace is too costly to wear every day. But I beseech your grace, pardon me. I was born to speak all mirth and no matter.

DON PEDRO Your silence most offends me, and to be merry

best becomes you; for out o' question, you were born in a merry hour.

BEATRICE No, sure, my lord, my mother cried. But then there was a star danced, and under that was I born.

Romeo and Juliet

Act I Scene 3

The Nurse remembers Juliet's infancy.

NURSE

Even or odd, of all days in the year
Come Lammas Eve at night shall she be fourteen.
Susan and she—God rest all Christian souls!—
Were of an age. Well, Susan is with God;
She was too good for me. But, as I said,
On Lammas Eve at night shall she be fourteen,
That shall she, marry, I remember it well.
'Tis since the earthquake now eleven years,
And she was weaned—I never shall forget it—
Of all the days of the year upon that day,
For I had then laid wormwood to my dug,
Sitting in the sun under the dovehouse wall.
My lord and you were then at Mantua.
Nay, I do bear a brain! But, as I said,
When it did taste the wormwood on the nipple
Of my dug and felt it bitter, pretty fool,
To see it tetchy and fall out wi'th' dug!

'Shake', quoth the dove-house! 'Twas no need, I trow,
To bid me trudge;
And since that time it is eleven years,
For then she could stand high-lone. Nay, by th' rood,
She could have run and waddled all about,
For even the day before, she broke her brow,
And then my husband—God be with his soul,
A was a merry man!—took up the child.
'Yea,' quoth he, 'dost thou fall upon thy face?
Thou wilt fall backward when thou hast more wit,
Wilt thou not, Jule?' And, by my halidom,
The pretty wretch left crying and said 'Ay'.
To see now how a jest shall come about!
I warrant an I should live a thousand years
I never should forget it. 'Wilt thou not, Jule?' quoth he,
And, pretty fool, it stinted and said 'Ay'.

CAPULET'S WIFE

Enough of this. I pray thee hold thy peace.

NURSE

Yes, madam. Yet I cannot choose but laugh
To think it should leave crying and say 'Ay'.
And yet, I warrant, it had upon it brow
A bump as big as a young cock'rel's stone.
A perilous knock, and it cried bitterly.
'Yea,' quoth my husband, 'fall'st upon thy face?
Thou wilt fall backward when thou com'st to age,
Wilt thou not, Jule?' It stinted and said 'Ay'.

JULIET

And stint thou too, I pray thee, Nurse, say I.

NURSE

Peace, I have done. God mark thee to his grace,

Thou wast the prettiest babe that e'er I nursed.
An I might live to see thee married once,
I have my wish.

Elizabeth Spriggs played Beatrice with the Royal Shakespeare Company in 1971 and the Nurse in 1967.

TOBY STEPHENS

✡

Coriolanus

Act III Scene 2

Coriolanus is urged by his mother, Volumnia and by the patricians Menenius and Cominius, to solicit the plebeians' votes.

CORIOLANUS

Must I go show them my unbarbèd sconce?
Must I with my base tongue give to my noble heart
A lie that it must bear? Well, I will do't.
Yet were there but this single plot to lose,
This mould of Martius they to dust should grind it
And throw't against the wind. To th' market-place.
You have put me now to such a part which never
I shall discharge to th' life.

COMINIUS Come, come, we'll prompt you.

VOLUMNIA

I prithee now, sweet son, as thou hast said
My praises made thee first a soldier, so,
To have my praise for this, perform a part
Thou hast not done before.

CORIOLANUS Well, I must do't.

Away, my disposition; and possess me
Some harlot's spirit! My throat of war be turned,

Which choired with my drum, into a pipe
Small as an eunuch or the virgin voice
That babies lull asleep! The smiles of knaves
Tent in my cheeks, and schoolboys' tears take up
The glasses of my sight! A beggar's tongue
Make motion through my lips, and my armed knees,
Who bowed but in my stirrup, bend like his
That hath received an alms!—I will not do't,
Lest I surcease to honour mine own truth,
And by my body's action teach my mind
A most inherent baseness.

VOLUMNIA At thy choice, then.
To beg of thee it is my more dishonour
Than thou of them. Come all to ruin. Let
Thy mother rather feel thy pride than fear
Thy dangerous stoutness, for I mock at death
With as big heart as thou. Do as thou list.
Thy valiantness was mine, thou sucked'st it from me,
But owe thy pride thyself.

CORIOLANUS Pray be content.
Mother, I am going to the market-place.
Chide me no more. I'll mountebank their loves,
Cog their hearts from them, and come home beloved
Of all the trades in Rome. Look, I am going.
Commend me to my wife. I'll return consul,
Or never trust to what my tongue can do
I'th' way of flattery further.

VOLUMNIA Do your will.

Exit Volumnia

COMINIUS
Away! The tribunes do attend you. Arm yourself

To answer mildly, for they are prepared
With accusations, as I hear, more strong
Than are upon you yet.

CORIOLANUS

The word is 'mildly'. Pray you let us go.
Let them accuse me by invention, I
Will answer in mine honour.

MENENIUS Ay, but mildly.

CORIOLANUS Well, mildly be it, then—mildly. *Exeunt*

Toby Stephens played Coriolanus with the Royal Shakespeare Company in 1994.

JULIET STEVENSON

✡

As You Like It

Act III Scene 2

In the forest Rosalind, disguised as a young man, with her cousin Celia meets Orlando, who is love-sick for the true Rosalind.

ROSALIND (*to Celia*) I will speak to him like a saucy lackey, and under that habit play the knave with him. (*To Orlando*) Do you hear, forester?

ORLANDO Very well. What would you?

ROSALIND I pray you, what is't o'clock?

ORLANDO You should ask me what time o' day. There's no clock in the forest.

ROSALIND Then there is no true lover in the forest, else sighing every minute and groaning every hour would detect the lazy foot of time as well as a clock.

ORLANDO And why not the swift foot of time? Had not that been as proper?

ROSALIND By no means, sir. Time travels in divers paces with divers persons. I'll tell you who time ambles withal, who time trots withal, who time gallops withal, and who he stands still withal.

ORLANDO I prithee, who doth he trot withal?

ROSALIND Marry, he trots hard with a young maid between

the contract of her marriage and the day it is solemnized. If the interim be but a se'nnight, time's pace is so hard that it seems the length of seven year.

ORLANDO Who ambles time withal?

ROSALIND With a priest that lacks Latin, and a rich man that hath not the gout; for the one sleeps easily because he cannot study, and the other lives merrily because he feels no pain, the one lacking the burden of lean and wasteful learning, the other knowing no burden of heavy tedious penury. These time ambles withal.

ORLANDO Who doth he gallop withal?

ROSALIND With a thief to the gallows; for though he go as softly as foot can fall, he thinks himself too soon there.

ORLANDO Who stays it still withal?

ROSALIND With lawyers in the vacation; for they sleep between term and term, and then they perceive not how time moves.

ORLANDO Where dwell you, pretty youth?

ROSALIND With this shepherdess, my sister, here in the skirts of the forest, like fringe upon a petticoat.

ORLANDO Are you native of this place?

ROSALIND As the coney that you see dwell where she is kindled.

ORLANDO Your accent is something finer than you could purchase in so removed a dwelling.

ROSALIND I have been told so of many; but indeed an old religious uncle of mine taught me to speak, who was in his youth an inland man; one that knew courtship too well, for there he fell in love. I have heard him read many lectures against it, and I thank God I am not a woman, to be touched with so many giddy offences as he hath generally taxed their whole sex withal.

ORLANDO Can you remember any of the principal evils that he laid to the charge of women?

ROSALIND There were none principal; they were all like one another as halfpence are, every one fault seeming monstrous till his fellow-fault came to match it.

ORLANDO I prithee, recount some of them.

ROSALIND No. I will not cast away my physic but on those that are sick. There is a man haunts the forest that abuses our young plants with carving Rosalind on their barks; hangs odes upon hawthorns and elegies on brambles; all, forsooth, deifying the name of Rosalind. If I could meet that fancy-monger, I would give him some good counsel, for he seems to have the quotidian of love upon him.

ORLANDO I am he that is so love-shaked. I pray you, tell me your remedy.

ROSALIND There is none of my uncle's marks upon you. He taught me how to know a man in love, in which cage of rushes I am sure you are not prisoner.

ORLANDO What were his marks?

ROSALIND A lean cheek, which you have not; a blue eye and sunken, which you have not; an unquestionable spirit, which you have not; a beard neglected, which you have not—but I pardon you for that, for simply your having in beard is a younger brother's revenue. Then your hose should be ungartered, your bonnet unbanded, your sleeve unbuttoned, your shoe untied, and everything about you demonstrating a careless desolation. But you are no such man. You are rather point-device in your accoutrements, as loving yourself than seeming the lover of any other.

ORLANDO Fair youth, I would I could make thee believe I love.

ROSALIND Me believe it? You may as soon make her that you love believe it, which I warrant she is apter to do than to confess she does. That is one of the points in the which women still give the lie to their consciences. But in good sooth, are you he that hangs the verses on the trees wherein Rosalind is so admired?

ORLANDO I swear to thee, youth, by the white hand of Rosalind, I am that he, that unfortunate he.

ROSALIND But are you so much in love as your rhymes speak?

ORLANDO Neither rhyme nor reason can express how much.

ROSALIND Love is merely a madness, and I tell you, deserves as well a dark house and a whip as madmen do; and the reason why they are not so punished and cured is that the lunacy is so ordinary that the whippers are in love too. Yet I profess curing it by counsel.

ORLANDO Did you ever cure any so?

ROSALIND Yes, one; and in this manner. He was to imagine me his love, his mistress; and I set him every day to woo me. At which time would I, being but a moonish youth, grieve, be effeminate, changeable, longing and liking, proud, fantastical, apish, shallow, inconstant, full of tears, full of smiles; for every passion something, and for no passion truly anything, as boys and women are for the most part cattle of this colour—would now like him, now loathe him; then entertain him, then forswear him; now weep for him, then spit at him, that I drave my suitor from his mad humour of love to a living humour of madness, which was to forswear the full stream of the world and to live in a nook merely monastic. And thus I cured him, and this way will I take upon me to wash your liver as clean as a sound sheep's heart, that there shall not be one spot of love in't.

ORLANDO I would not be cured, youth.

ROSALIND I would cure you if you would but call me Rosalind and come every day to my cot, and woo me.

ORLANDO Now by the faith of my love, I will. Tell me where it is.

ROSALIND Go with me to it, and I'll show it you. And by the way you shall tell me where in the forest you live. Will you go?

ORLANDO With all my heart, good youth.

ROSALIND Nay, you must call me Rosalind.—Come, sister. Will you go? *Exeunt*

Juliet Stevenson played Rosalind with the Royal Shakespeare Company in 1985.

DAVID SUCHET

✡

The Tempest

Act III Scene 2

Overlooked by the invisible Ariel, Caliban plots Prospero's murder with Stephano and Trinculo.

CALIBAN

Why, as I told thee, 'tis a custom with him
I'th' afternoon to sleep. There thou mayst brain him,
Having first seized his books; or with a log
Batter his skull, or paunch him with a stake,
Or cut his weasand with thy knife. Remember
First to possess his books, for without them
He's but a sot as I am, nor hath not
One spirit to command—they all do hate him
As rootedly as I. Burn but his books.
He has brave utensils, for so he calls them,
Which when he has a house he'll deck withal.
And that most deeply to consider is
The beauty of his daughter. He himself
Calls her a nonpareil. I never saw a woman
But only Sycorax my dam and she,
But she as far surpasseth Sycorax
As great'st does least.

STEPHANO Is it so brave a lass?

CALIBAN
Ay, lord. She will become thy bed, I warrant,
And bring thee forth brave brood.

STEPHANO Monster, I will kill this man. His daughter and I will be king and queen—save our graces!—and Trinculo and thyself shall be viceroys. Dost thou like the plot, Trinculo?

TRINCULO Excellent.

STEPHANO Give me thy hand. I am sorry I beat thee. But while thou liv'st, keep a good tongue in thy head.

CALIBAN
Within this half hour will he be asleep.
Wilt thou destroy him then?

STEPHANO Ay, on mine honour.

ARIEL (*aside*) This will I tell my master.

CALIBAN
Thou mak'st me merry; I am full of pleasure.
Let us be jocund. Will you troll the catch
You taught me but while-ere?

STEPHANO At thy request, monster, I will do reason, any reason.—Come on, Trinculo, let us sing.

(*Sings*) Flout 'em and cout 'em,
And scout 'em and flout 'em.
Thought is free.

CALIBAN That's not the tune.

Ariel plays the tune on a tabor and pipe

STEPHANO What is this same?

TRINCULO This is the tune of our catch, played by the picture of Nobody.

STEPHANO (*calls towards Ariel*) If thou beest a man, show thyself in thy likeness. If thou beest a devil, take't as thou list.

TRINCULO O, forgive me my sins!

STEPHANO He that dies pays all debts. (*Calls*) I defy thee.—
Mercy upon us!

CALIBAN Art thou afeard?

STEPHANO No, monster, not I.

CALIBAN

Be not afeard. The isle is full of noises,
Sounds, and sweet airs, that give delight and hurt not.
Sometimes a thousand twangling instruments
Will hum about mine ears, and sometime voices
That if I then had waked after long sleep
Will make me sleep again; and then in dreaming
The clouds methought would open and show riches
Ready to drop upon me, that when I waked
I cried to dream again.

STEPHANO This will prove a brave kingdom to me, where I shall have my music for nothing.

CALIBAN When Prospero is destroyed.

STEPHANO That shall be by and by. I remember the story.

Exit Ariel, playing music

TRINCULO The sound is going away. Let's follow it, and after do our work.

STEPHANO Lead, monster; we'll follow.—I would I could see this taborer. He lays it on.

TRINCULO (*to Caliban*) Wilt come? I'll follow Stefano.

Exeunt

David Suchet played Caliban with the Royal Shakespeare Company in 1978.

JANET SUZMAN

✡

The Taming of the Shrew

Act II Scene 1

Petruchio, in search of a rich wife, meets the shrewish Katherina

PETRUCHIO ... I'll attend her here,
And woo her with some spirit when she comes.
Say that she rail, why then I'll tell her plain
She sings as sweetly as a nightingale.
Say that she frown, I'll say she looks as clear
As morning roses newly washed with dew.
Say she be mute and will not speak a word,
Then I'll commend her volubility,
And say she uttereth piercing eloquence.
If she do bid me pack, I'll give her thanks
As though she bid me stay by her a week.
If she deny to wed, I'll crave the day
When I shall ask the banns, and when be marrièd.
But here she comes, and now, Petruchio, speak.
Enter Katherina
Good morrow, Kate, for that's your name, I hear.

KATHERINE
Well have you heard, but something hard of hearing.
They call me Katherine that do talk of me.

PETRUCHIO

You lie, in faith, for you are called plain Kate,
And bonny Kate, and sometimes Kate the curst,
But Kate, the prettiest Kate in Christendom,
Kate of Kate Hall, my super-dainty Kate—
For dainties are all cates, and therefore 'Kate'—
Take this of me, Kate of my consolation:
Hearing thy mildness praised in every town,
Thy virtues spoke of, and thy beauty sounded—
Yet not so deeply as to thee belongs—
Myself am moved to woo thee for my wife.

KATHERINE

Moved? In good time. Let him that moved you hither
Re-move you hence. I knew you at the first
You were a movable.

PETRUCHIO Why, what's a movable?

KATHERINE

A joint-stool.

PETRUCHIO Thou hast hit it. Come, sit on me.

KATHERINE

Asses are made to bear, and so are you.

PETRUCHIO

Women are made to bear, and so are you.

KATHERINE

No such jade as you, if me you mean.

PETRUCHIO

Alas, good Kate, I will not burden thee,
For knowing thee to be but young and light.

KATHERINE

Too light for such a swain as you to catch,
And yet as heavy as my weight should be.

PETRUCHIO
Should be?—should buzz.
KATHERINE Well ta'en, and like a buzzard.
PETRUCHIO
O slow-winged turtle, shall a buzzard take thee?
KATHERINE
Ay, for a turtle, as he takes a buzzard.
PETRUCHIO
Come, come, you wasp, i'faith you are too angry.
KATHERINE
If I be waspish, best beware my sting.
PETRUCHIO
My remedy is then to pluck it out.
KATHERINE
Ay, if the fool could find it where it lies.
PETRUCHIO
Who knows not where a wasp does wear his sting?
In his tail.
KATHERINE In his tongue.
PETRUCHIO Whose tongue?
KATHERINE
Yours, if you talk of tales, and so farewell.
PETRUCHIO
What, with my tongue in your tail? Nay, come again,
Good Kate, I am a gentleman.
KATHERINE That I'll try.
She strikes him
PETRUCHIO
I swear I'll cuff you if you strike again.
KATHERINE So may you lose your arms.
If you strike me you are no gentleman,

And if no gentleman, why then, no arms.

PETRUCHIO

A herald, Kate? O, put me in thy books.

KATHERINE

What is your crest—a coxcomb?

PETRUCHIO

A combless cock, so Kate will be my hen.

KATHERINE

No cock of mine. You crow too like a craven.

PETRUCHIO

Nay, come, Kate, come. You must not look so sour.

KATHERINE

It is my fashion when I see a crab.

PETRUCHIO

Why, here's no crab, and therefore look not sour.

KATHERINE There is, there is.

PETRUCHIO Then show it me.

KATHERINE Had I a glass I would.

PETRUCHIO

What, you mean my face?

KATHERINE Well aimed, of such a young one.

PETRUCHIO

Now, by Saint George, I am too young for you.

KATHERINE

Yet you are withered.

PETRUCHIO 'Tis with cares.

KATHERINE I care not.

PETRUCHIO

Nay, hear you, Kate. In sooth, you scape not so.

KATHERINE

I chafe you if I tarry. Let me go.

PETRUCHIO No, not a whit. I find you passing gentle.
'Twas told me you were rough, and coy, and sullen,
And now I find report a very liar,
For thou art pleasant, gamesome, passing courteous,
But slow in speech, yet sweet as springtime flowers.
Thou canst not frown. Thou canst not look askance,
Nor bite the lip, as angry wenches will,
Nor hast thou pleasure to be cross in talk,
But thou with mildness entertain'st thy wooers,
With gentle conference, soft, and affable.
Why does the world report that Kate doth limp?
O sland'rous world! Kate like the hazel twig
Is straight and slender, and as brown in hue
As hazelnuts, and sweeter than the kernels.
O let me see thee walk. Thou dost not halt.

KATHERINE
Go, fool, and whom thou keep'st command.

PETRUCHIO
Did ever Dian so become a grove
As Kate this chamber with her princely gait?
O, be thou Dian, and let her be Kate,
And then let Kate be chaste and Dian sportful.

KATHERINE
Where did you study all this goodly speech?

PETRUCHIO
It is extempore, from my mother-wit.

KATHERINE
A witty mother, witless else her son.

PETRUCHIO
Am I not wise?

KATHERINE Yes, keep you warm.

PETRUCHIO

Marry, so I mean, sweet Katherine, in thy bed.
And therefore setting all this chat aside,
Thus in plain terms: your father hath consented
That you shall be my wife, your dowry 'greed on,
And will you, nill you, I will marry you.
Now, Kate, I am a husband for your turn,
For by this light, whereby I see thy beauty—
Thy beauty that doth make me like thee well—
Thou must be married to no man but me,
Enter Baptista, Gremio, and Tranio as Lucentio
For I am he am born to tame you, Kate,
And bring you from a wild Kate to a Kate
Conformable as other household Kates.
Here comes your father. Never make denial.
I must and will have Katherine to my wife.

Janet Suzman played Katherina with the Royal Shakespeare Company in 1967.

DOROTHY TUTIN

✡

Twelfth Night

Act II Scene 4

Viola, disguised as a boy, Cesario, is serving Duke Orsino, whom she loves. He wishes her to further his suit to Olivia.

ORSINO ... Once more, Cesario,
Get thee to yon same sovereign cruelty.
Tell her my love, more noble than the world,
Prizes not quantity of dirty lands.
The parts that fortune hath bestowed upon her
Tell her I hold as giddily as fortune;
But 'tis that miracle and queen of gems
That nature pranks her in attracts my soul.

VIOLA
But if she cannot love you, sir?

ORSINO
I cannot be so answered.

VIOLA Sooth, but you must.
Say that some lady, as perhaps there is,
Hath for your love as great a pang of heart
As you have for Olivia. You cannot love her.
You tell her so. Must she not then be answered?

ORSINO
There is no woman's sides

Can bide the beating of so strong a passion
As love doth give my heart; no woman's heart
So big, to hold so much. They lack retention.
Alas, their love may be called appetite,
No motion of the liver, but the palate,
That suffer surfeit, cloyment, and revolt.
But mine is all as hungry as the sea,
And can digest as much. Make no compare
Between that love a woman can bear me
And that I owe Olivia.

VIOLA Ay, but I know—

ORSINO
What dost thou know?

VIOLA
Too well what love women to men may owe.
In faith, they are as true of heart as we.
My father had a daughter loved a man
As it might be, perhaps, were I a woman
I should your lordship.

ORSINO And what's her history?

VIOLA
A blank, my lord. She never told her love,
But let concealment, like a worm i'th' bud,
Feed on her damask cheek. She pined in thought,
And with a green and yellow melancholy
She sat like patience on a monument,
Smiling at grief. Was not this love indeed?
We men may say more, swear more, but indeed
Our shows are more than will; for still we prove
Much in our vows, but little in our love.

ORSINO
But died thy sister of her love, my boy?

VIOLA
I am all the daughters of my father's house,
And all the brothers too; and yet I know not.
Sir, shall I to this lady?
ORSINO Ay, that's the theme,
To her in haste. Give her this jewel. Say
My love can give no place, bide no denay.
Exeunt separately

Dorothy Tutin played Viola at the Shakespeare Memorial Theatre in 1958.

PHILIP VOSS

✡

Coriolanus

Act I Scene 1

The starving Roman citizens are rioting. Menenius, a patrician, tries to pacify them.

MENENIUS

There was a time when all the body's members,
Rebelled against the belly, thus accused it:
That only like a gulf it did remain
I'th' midst o'th' body, idle and unactive,
Still cupboarding the viand, never bearing
Like labour with the rest; where th'other instruments
Did see and hear, devise, instruct, walk, feel,
And, mutually participate, did minister
Unto the appetite and affection common
Of the whole body. The belly answered—

FIRST CITIZEN

Well, sir, what answer made the belly?

MENENIUS

Sir, I shall tell you. With a kind of smile,
Which ne'er came from the lungs, but even thus—
For look you, I may make the belly smile
As well as speak—it tauntingly replied

To th' discontented members, the mutinous parts
That envied his receipt; even so most fitly
As you malign our senators for that
They are not such as you.

FIRST CITIZEN Your belly's answer—what?
The kingly crownèd head, the vigilant eye,
The counsellor heart, the arm our soldier,
Our steed the leg, the tongue our trumpeter,
With other muniments and petty helps
In this our fabric, if that they—

MENENIUS What then?
Fore me, this fellow speaks! What then? What then?

FIRST CITIZEN
Should by the cormorant belly be restrained,
Who is the sink o'th' body—

MENENIUS Well, what then?

FIRST CITIZEN
The former agents, if they did complain,
What could the belly answer?

MENENIUS I will tell you,
If you'll bestow a small of what you have little—
Patience—a while, you'st hear the belly's answer.

FIRST CITIZEN
You're long about it.

MENENIUS Note me this, good friend:
Your most grave belly was deliberate,
Not rash like his accusers, and thus answered:
'True is it, my incorporate friends,' quoth he,
'That I receive the general food at first
Which you do live upon, and fit it is,
Because I am the storehouse and the shop

Of the whole body. But, if you do remember,
I send it through the rivers of your blood
Even to the court, the heart, to th' seat o'th' brain;
And through the cranks and offices of man
The strongest nerves and small inferior veins
From me receive that natural competency
Whereby they live. And though that all at once'—
You my good friends, this says the belly, mark me—

FIRST CITIZEN
Ay, sir, well, well.

MENENIUS 'Though all at once cannot
See what I do deliver out to each,
Yet I can make my audit up that all
From me do back receive the flour of all
And leave me but the bran.' What say you to't?

FIRST CITIZEN
It was an answer. How apply you this?

MENENIUS
The senators of Rome are this good belly,
And you the mutinous members. For examine
Their counsels and their cares, digest things rightly
Touching the weal o'th' common, you shall find
No public benefit which you receive
But it proceeds or comes from them to you,
And no way from yourselves.

The Tempest

Act IV Scene 1

The masque conjured up by Prospero for his daughter Miranda and her betrothed Ferdinand has vanished.

PROSPERO

You do look, my son, in a moved sort,
As if you were dismayed. Be cheerful, sir.
Our revels now are ended. These our actors,
As I foretold you, were all spirits, and
Are melted into air, into thin air;
And like the baseless fabric of this vision,
The cloud-capped towers, the gorgeous palaces,
The solemn temples, the great globe itself,
Yea, all which it inherit, shall dissolve;
And, like this insubstantial pageant faded,
Leave not a rack behind. We are such stuff
As dreams are made on, and our little life
Is rounded with a sleep. Sir, I am vexed.
Bear with my weakness. My old brain is troubled.
Be not disturbed with my infirmity.
If you be pleased, retire into my cell,
And there repose. A turn or two I'll walk
To still my beating mind.

Philip Voss played Menenius with the Royal Shakespeare Company in 1994.

HARRIET WALTER

✡

All's Well that Ends Well

Act I Scene 1

Helena, a poor physician's daughter, has fallen in love with Bertram, Count of Roussillon. She hopes she may win him by curing the King's disease.

Our remedies oft in ourselves do lie
Which we ascribe to heaven. The fated sky
Gives us free scope, only doth backward pull
Our slow designs when we ourselves are dull.
What power is it which mounts my love so high,
That makes me see and cannot feed mine eye?
The mightiest space in fortune nature brings
To join like likes and kiss like native things.
Impossible be strange attempts to those
That weigh their pains in sense and do suppose
What hath been cannot be. Who ever strove
To show her merit that did miss her love?
The King's disease—my project may deceive me,
But my intents are fixed and will not leave me.

Henry IV, Part Two

Act II Scene 3

Lady Percy, Hotspur's widow, tries to persuade her father-in-law, the Earl of Northumberland, not to go to the wars

O yet, for God's sake, go not to these wars!
The time was, father, that you broke your word
When you were more endeared to it than now—
When your own Percy, when my heart's dear Harry,
Threw many a northward look to see his father
Bring up his powers; but he did long in vain.
Who then persuaded you to stay at home?
There were two honours lost, yours and your son's.
For yours, the God of heaven brighten it!
For his, it stuck upon him as the sun
In the grey vault of heaven, and by his light
Did all the chivalry of England move
To do brave acts. He was indeed the glass
Wherein the noble youth did dress themselves.
He had no legs that practised not his gait;
And speaking thick, which nature made his blemish,
Became the accents of the valiant;
For those that could speak low and tardily
Would turn their own perfection to abuse
To seem like him. So that in speech, in gait,
In diet, in affections of delight,
In military rules, humours of blood,
He was the mark and glass, copy and book,

That fashioned others. And him—O wondrous him!
O miracle of men!—him did you leave,
Second to none, unseconded by you,
To look upon the hideous god of war
In disadvantage, to abide a field
Where nothing but the sound of Hotspur's name
Did seem defensible; so you left him.
Never, O never do his ghost the wrong
To hold your honour more precise and nice
With others than with him. Let them alone.
The Marshal and the Archbishop are strong.
Had my sweet Harry had but half their numbers,
Today might I, hanging on Hotspur's neck,
Have talked of Monmouth's grave.

Harriet Walter played Helena and Lady Percy with the Royal Shakespeare Company in 1981.

ZOË WANAMAKER

✡

Twelfth Night

Act III Scene 1

Viola, disguised as the page Cesario, meets Feste the jester.

VIOLA Save thee, friend, and thy music. Dost thou live by thy tabor?

FESTE No, sir, I live by the church.

VIOLA Art thou a churchman?

FESTE No such matter, sir. I do live by the church for I do live at my house, and my house doth stand by the church.

VIOLA So thou mayst say the king lies by a beggar if a beggar dwell near him, or the church stands by thy tabor if thy tabor stand by the church.

FESTE You have said, sir. To see this age!—A sentence is but a cheverel glove to a good wit, how quickly the wrong side may be turned outward.

VIOLA Nay, that's certain. They that dally nicely with words may quickly make them wanton.

FESTE I would therefore my sister had had no name, sir.

VIOLA Why, man?

FESTE Why, sir, her name's a word, and to dally with that word might make my sister wanton. But indeed, words are very rascals since bonds disgraced them.

VIOLA Thy reason, man?

FESTE Troth, sir, I can yield you none without words, and words are grown so false I am loath to prove reason with them.

VIOLA I warrant thou art a merry fellow, and carest for nothing.

FESTE Not so, sir, I do care for something; but in my conscience, sir, I do not care for you. If that be to care for nothing, sir, I would it would make you invisible.

VIOLA Art not thou the Lady Olivia's fool?

FESTE No indeed, sir, the Lady Olivia has no folly, she will keep no fool, sir, till she be married, and fools are as like husbands as pilchards are to herrings—the husband's the bigger. I am indeed not her fool, but her corrupter of words.

VIOLA I saw thee late at the Count Orsino's.

FESTE Foolery, sir, does walk about the orb like the sun, it shines everywhere. I would be sorry, sir, but the fool should be as oft with your master as with my mistress. I think I saw your wisdom there.

VIOLA Nay, an thou pass upon me, I'll no more with thee. (*Giving money*) Hold, there's expenses for thee.

FESTE Now Jove in his next commodity of hair send thee a beard.

VIOLA By my troth I'll tell thee, I am almost sick for one, though I would not have it grow on my chin. Is thy lady within?

FESTE Would not a pair of these have bred, sir?

VIOLA Yes, being kept together and put to use.

FESTE I would play Lord Pandarus of Phrygia, sir, to bring a Cressida to this Troilus.

VIOLA (*giving money*) I understand you, sir, 'tis well begged.

FESTE The matter I hope is not great, sir; begging but a beggar—Cressida was a beggar. My lady is within, sir. I will conster to them whence you come. Who you are and what you would are out of my welkin—I might say 'element', but the word is over-worn. *Exit*

VIOLA

This fellow is wise enough to play the fool,
And to do that well craves a kind of wit.
He must observe their mood on whom he jests,
The quality of persons, and the time,
And, like the haggard, check at every feather
That comes before his eye. This is a practice
As full of labour as a wise man's art,
For folly that he wisely shows is fit,
But wise men, folly-fall'n, quite taint their wit.

Enter Sir Toby and Sir Andrew

Zoë Wanamaker played Viola with the Royal Shakespeare Company in 1983.

MICHAEL WILLIAMS

✡

The Winter's Tale

Act IV Scene 3

The tinker Autocylus encounters a country bumpkin on his way to buy provisions for a sheepshearing feast.

Enter Autolycus singing

AUTOLYCUS

When daffodils begin to peer,
With heigh, the doxy over the dale,
Why then comes in the sweet o'the year,
For the red blood reigns in the winter's pale.

The white sheet bleaching on the hedge,
With heigh, the sweet birds, O how they sing!
Doth set my pugging tooth on edge,
For a quart of ale is a dish for a king.

The lark, that tirra-lirra chants,
With heigh, with heigh, the thrush and the jay,
Are summer songs for me and my aunts
While we lie tumbling in the hay.

I have served Prince Florizel, and in my time wore three-pile, but now I am out of service.

But shall I go mourn for that, my dear?
The pale moon shines by night,
And when I wander here and there
I then do most go right.

If tinkers may have leave to live,
And bear the sow-skin budget,
Then my account I well may give,
And in the stocks avouch it.

My traffic is sheets. When the kite builds, look to lesser linen. My father named me Autolycus, who being, as I am, littered under Mercury, was likewise a snapper-up of unconsidered trifles. With die and drab I purchased this caparison, and my revenue is the silly cheat. Gallows and knock are too powerful on the highway. Beating and hanging are terrors to me. For the life to come, I sleep out the thought of it. A prize, a prize!

Enter Clown

CLOWN Let me see. Every 'leven wether tods, every tod yields pound and odd shilling. Fifteen hundred shorn, what comes the wool to?

AUTOLYCUS (*aside*) If the springe hold, the cock's mine.

CLOWN I cannot do't without counters. Let me see, what am I to buy for our sheep-shearing feast? Three pound of sugar, five pound of currants, rice—what will this sister of mine do with rice? But my father hath made her mistress of the feast, and she lays it on. She hath made me four-and-twenty nosegays for the shearers—three-man-song-men, all, and very good ones—but they are most of them means and basses, but one Puritan amongst them, and he sings psalms to hornpipes. I must have saffron to colour the warden pies;

mace; dates, none—that's out of my note; nutmegs, seven; a race or two of ginger—but that I may beg; four pound of prunes, and as many of raisins o'th' sun.

AUTOLYCUS (*grovelling on the ground*) O, that ever I was born!

CLOWN I'th' name of me!

AUTOLYCUS O help me, help me! Pluck but off these rags, and then death, death!

CLOWN Alack, poor soul, thou hast need of more rags to lay on thee rather than have these off.

AUTOLYCUS O sir, the loathsomeness of them offend me more than the stripes I have received, which are mighty ones and millions.

CLOWN Alas, poor man, a million of beating may come to a great matter.

AUTOLYCUS I am robbed, sir, and beaten; my money and apparel ta'en from me, and these detestable things put upon me.

CLOWN What, by a horseman, or a footman?

AUTOLYCUS A footman, sweet sir, a footman.

CLOWN Indeed, he should be a footman, by the garments he has left with thee. If this be a horseman's coat it hath seen very hot service. Lend me thy hand, I'll help thee. Come, lend me thy hand.

He helps Autolycus up

AUTOLYCUS O, good sir, tenderly. O!

CLOWN Alas, poor soul!

AUTOLYCUS O, good sir, softly, good sir! I fear, sir, my shoulder-blade is out.

CLOWN How now? Canst stand?

AUTOLYCUS Softly, dear sir. Good sir, softly.

He picks the Clown's pocket

You ha' done me a charitable office.

CLOWN (*reaching for his purse*) Dost lack any money? I have a little money for thee.

AUTOLYCUS No, good sweet sir, no, I beseech you, sir. I have a kinsman not past three-quarters of a mile hence, unto whom I was going. I shall there have money, or anything I want. Offer me no money, I pray you. That kills my heart.

CLOWN What manner of fellow was he that robbed you?

AUTOLYCUS A fellow, sir, that I have known to go about with troll-madams. I knew him once a servant of the Prince. I cannot tell, good sir, for which of his virtues it was, but he was certainly whipped out of the court.

CLOWN His vices, you would say. There's no virtue whipped out of the court. They cherish it to make it stay there; and yet it will no more but abide.

AUTOLYCUS Vices, I would say, sir. I know this man well. He hath been since an ape-bearer, then a process-server—a bailiff—then he compassed a motion of the Prodigal Son, and married a tinker's wife within a mile where my land and living lies, and having flown over many knavish professions, he settled only in rogue. Some call him Autolycus.

CLOWN Out upon him! Prig, for my life, prig! He haunts wakes, fairs, and bear-baitings.

AUTOLYCUS Very true, sir. He, sir, he. That's the rogue that put me into this apparel.

CLOWN Not a more cowardly rogue in all Bohemia. If you had but looked big and spit at him, he'd have run.

AUTOLYCUS I must confess to you, sir, I am no fighter. I am false of heart that way, and that he knew, I warrant him.

CLOWN How do you now?

AUTOLYCUS Sweet sir, much better than I was. I can stand,

and walk. I will even take my leave of you, and pace softly towards my kinsman's.

CLOWN Shall I bring thee on the way?

AUTOLYCUS No, good-faced sir, no, sweet sir.

CLOWN Then fare thee well. I must go buy spices for our sheep-shearing.

AUTOLYCUS Prosper you, sweet sir.

Exit the Clown

Your purse is not hot enough to purchase your spice. I'll be with you at your sheep-shearing, too. If I make not this cheat bring out another, and the shearers prove sheep, let me be unrolled and my name put in the book of virtue.

(*Sings*) Jog on, jog on, the footpath way,
And merrily hent the stile-a.
A merry heart goes all the day,
Your sad tires in a mile-a.

King Lear

Act I Scene 5

As Lear muses on his daughter Goneril's ingratitude, his Fool desperately tries to amuse him.

FOOL If a man's brains were in's heels, were't not in danger of kibes?

LEAR Ay, boy.

FOOL Then, I prithee, be merry: thy wit shall not go slipshod.

LEAR Ha, ha, ha!

FOOL Shalt see thy other daughter will use thee kindly, for though she's as like this as a crab's like an apple, yet I can tell what I can tell.

LEAR What canst tell, boy?

FOOL She will taste as like this as a crab does to a crab. Thou canst tell why one's nose stands i'th' middle on 's face?

LEAR No.

FOOL Why, to keep one's eyes of either side 's nose, that what a man cannot smell out, a may spy into.

LEAR I did her wrong.

FOOL Canst tell how an oyster makes his shell?

LEAR No.

FOOL Nor I neither; but I can tell why a snail has a house.

LEAR Why?

FOOL Why, to put 's head in, not to give it away to his daughters and leave his horns without a case.

LEAR I will forget my nature. So kind a father!
Be my horses ready?

FOOL Thy asses are gone about 'em. The reason why the seven stars are no more than seven is a pretty reason.

LEAR Because they are not eight.

FOOL Yes, indeed, thou wouldst make a good fool.

LEAR To take't again perforce—monster ingratitude!

FOOL If thou wert my fool, nuncle, I'd have thee beaten for being old before thy time.

LEAR How's that?

FOOL Thou shouldst not have been old till thou hadst been wise.

LEAR O, let me not be mad, not mad, sweet heaven!
Keep me in temper. I would not be mad.

Enter the First Gentleman

How now, are the horses ready?

FIRST GENTLEMAN Ready, my lord.

LEAR (*to Fool*) Come, boy.

Exeunt Lear and Gentleman

FOOL

She that's a maid now, and laughs at my departure,
Shall not be a maid long, unless things be cut shorter.

Exit

Michael Williams played Autocylus with the Royal Shakespeare Company in 1976, and the Fool in 1968 and 1976.